at the Kings Arms in St Pauls Church Yard London.

THE CITY OF HEREFORD.

The River Wye

A Pictorial History

Taking water from the Wye at Putson, near Hereford, c.1912.

The River Wye

A Pictorial History

Josephine Jeremiah

Phillimore

2004

Published by
PHILLIMORE & CO. LTD,
Shopwyke Manor Barn, Chichester, West Sussex, England

ISBN 1 86077 301 X

Printed and bound in Great Britain by
THE CROMWELL PRESS LTD
Trowbridge, Wiltshire

List of Illustrations

Frontispiece: Taking water from the Wye at Putson, near Hereford, *c.*1912

Acknowledgements

My thanks go to the following for their help in enabling me to compile this book:
Archive CD Books, Evesham Library and Ian Jeremiah.

Map of the River Wye

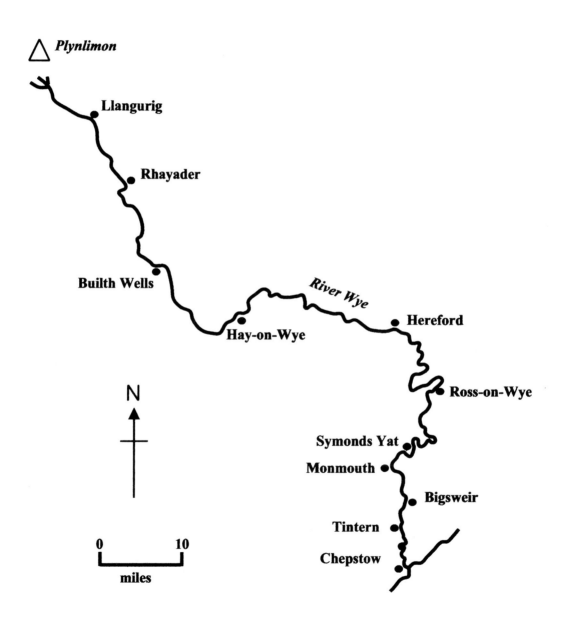

An Historical Journey

The Welsh mountain **Plynlimon**, rising to over 2,000ft., is the source not only of the River Wye, but of the rivers Severn and Rheidol too. Victorian author Leitch Ritchie described the start of the Wye as 'a tiny pool, little more than a hand-breadth across, supplied by droppings rather than gushes from a bank of black earth'. Robert Gibbings, well known for his book *Coming Down the Wye* (1942), depicted it as 'a pool no bigger than a bowler hat'. A.G. Bradley, in *The Wye* (1926), noted, 'it breaks into the world, a tiny rill, in such a fashion as to set all the bards singing'.

On the first stage of its journey, the rocky mountain stream bounds down through wild and rugged terrain to Llangurig, the first village on its banks. Then, tumbling through impressive upland scenery, the Wye descends to the market towns of Rhayader and Builth Wells, increasing in size. Just after Hay-on-Wye, the river comes to the border between Wales and England. The second stage of its passage takes it through a wide flood plain and then on to the cathedral city of Hereford. Gliding past lovely countryside, the Wye makes several great loops to Ross-on-Wye, once a starting point for 'The Wye Tour'. The third and most celebrated stage of the journey is along deep wooded gorges with spectacular views, like those at Symonds Yat. Passing the historic town of Monmouth, the Wye meanders towards the famous Cistercian abbey of Tintern. Finally, it flows through magnificent scenery to Chepstow before uniting with the River Severn.

The River Wye has been a venue for visitors for over two centuries. Dr John Egerton, an 18th-century rector of Ross, made 'The Wye Tour' popular when he took guests for boat trips down the river. In 1770, William Gilpin, Prebendary of Salisbury and Vicar of Boldre, near Lymington, made a journey from Ross to Chepstow in a covered boat navigated by three men. His object was to examine the scenery 'by the rules of picturesque beauty', which meant judging a spectacular view by a complicated set of rules before it could be deemed 'picturesque'. William Gilpin's book, *Observations on the River Wye and several parts of South Wales, &c. relative chiefly to Picturesque Beauty*, was first published in 1782. It was illustrated by a set of aquatints, which were produced to look like watercolours, the process involved using acid to bite into a printing plate to varying depths.

1 Picturesque beauty from William Gilpin's *Observations on the Wye*, 1800. The author used a new set of etchings in the fifth edition of his book as the old plates were too much worn to be of further use.

Samuel Ireland was a late 18th-century author and artist who used aquatints to illustrate his work. In 1794, he travelled down the river from its source, sketching suitable locations for his *Picturesque Views on the River Wye*, which was published in 1797. A year after his trip, a great flood devastated the country nationwide. The author wrote:

> The tremendous floods, which, in the beginning of the year 1795, subsequent to that in which these drawings were made, having so completely swept away several ancient, as well as elegant structures thrown across this stream, may perhaps give some additional value to the sketches of them here introduced.

Just over two centuries ago, William Coxe, Rector of Bemerton and Stourton, took a boat from Ross to Chepstow. He wrote, 'We embarked at seven in the morning in a convenient vessel, capable of containing eight persons, besides the boatmen, and provided with an awning, which as the weather was cloudy and sultry, we found a good defence against the rays of an August sun.' Often referred to as Archdeacon Coxe, he included two chapters on the 'Navigation of the Wy' in his work entitled *An Historical Tour in Monmouthshire*, which was published in two parts in 1801. Among other engravings, it was illustrated with views by Sir R.C. Hoare, his companion on the trip downriver.

Further description of boats, used in 'The Wye Tour' from Ross, may be found in *The Excursion down the Wye from Ross to Monmouth* by Charles Heath, which, by 1826, was in its eighth edition. The author commented, 'Boats lightly constructed, which are used either with or without sail, and navigated by three men, are kept in constant readiness.' He noted that the price of a boat from Ross to Monmouth was one guinea and a half, while from Ross to Chepstow it was three guineas. This was 'besides provisions for the Boatmen; which may be allowed for, or found by the company, as is most agreeable to the party'.

Taking a boat at Ross, the 19th-century author, Thomas Roscoe, observed:

> My 'light bark' was not much unlike a gondola, when its tarpauling cover was spread over the framework; but being favoured by a radiantly bright morning, I preferred sitting under the skeleton and enjoying the charming scenes around me. A table in the centre of the part allotted to passengers, and cushioned seats around, made this small floating parlour a most commodious conveyance.

Thomas Roscoe described his journey along the Wye in *Wanderings and Excursions in South Wales including the Scenery of the River Wye*, which dates from the 1830s. This book was illustrated with engravings by W. Radclyffe from drawings by Cox, Fielding, Creswick and Watson. Louisa Anne Twamley used the same engravings of the Wye and its surroundings for her book, *An Autumn Ramble by the Wye* (1839), plus a vignette plate of the 'View from Goodrich Old Court' on the title page. Her work differed from other descriptions of journeys down the river as the authoress wrote an account of her travels upstream from Chepstow to the source of the Wye. At Monmouth, bound for Ross, she took a boat 'which looked as if it wished to be taken for a gondola's fifteenth cousin … with commodious seats around the "company" end, and a table in the midst'. The authoress added, 'A keen, honest and intelligent old man was our "Skipper," and his two "helps" were as strong, stout young Welshmen as need be.'

Another book concerning the river was *The Wye and its Associations: A Picturesque Ramble* by Leitch Ritchie. This was published in 1841 and had 12 plates produced from drawings by T. Creswick. The author felt that, despite the publication of other descriptions of the Wye, something more was due on the subject that was 'not too large for the pocket, and yet aspiring to a place in the library'. Twenty years later, a guidebook written by Mr and Mrs S.C. Hall, entitled *The Book of South Wales, the Wye and the Coast*, was illustrated by engravings made from drawings by a number of artists. The authors wrote:

> Excellent boats, well and carefully manned, are to be obtained either at Hereford, Ross or Monmouth: The charges are somewhat high, necessarily so, considering the heavy labour attendant on "the return". For a boat with one man, the charge from Ross to Monmouth is 15s., the distance being twenty-three miles; for a larger boat, with two men, the charge is 30s. When the lighter boat is used, the boatman finds it easier to bring it back by land, on a truck, the distance being only ten miles; when the heavier boat makes the voyage the men are compelled

2 Man carrying a coracle near Ross, 1861.

to draw it along the shore, the difficulty of rowing upstream being (as we have intimated) very great, in consequence of the extreme rapidity of the current.

On the Wye, there were numerous shallows and rapids so trading craft had to be hauled upstream by gangs of men. These vessels, transporting goods up and downriver, were flat-bottomed barges and trows. The latter were open shallow-draughted sailing vessels, which also operated on the River Severn and its navigable tributaries. Wye trows were similar in design to Severn trows, but tended to be smaller. As can be imagined, hauling vessels up the river was extremely hard work.

There had been attempts in the 17th and 18th centuries to improve navigation on the Wye. The Rivers Wye and Lugg Navigation Act of 1662 authorised Sir William Sandys, who had improved the Avon Navigation, to build pound locks on the river. However, according to Charles Hadfield, in *The Canals of South Wales and the Border* (1977), weirs and flash locks were likely to have been built rather than pound locks. Over the years, these fell into disrepair. In 1695, an Act of Parliament appointed Commissioners to improve navigation by removing weirs. These were a constant bone of contention between river traders and those who maintained the weirs for either mill or fishing purposes. A number of the old weirs were destroyed, but the result was that there was often a lack of water in the river and great shoals occurred, hindering navigation. Another unsuccessful scheme was put forward, in 1763, to improve the navigation as far as Hereford with 22 locks to be built at a cost of £20,900. Samuel Ireland, writing in the mid-1790s about attempts to remove the barriers to navigation, was of the opinion that 'the estimate of expenses has been so enormous, that the measure has always proved abortive'.

In 1801, William Coxe observed, 'From Lidbrook large quantities of coal are sent to Ross and Hereford; and we passed several barges towed by ten or eleven men, which by great exertions are drawn to Hereford in two days.' By 1811, a horse towing-path had been constructed from Lydbrook to Hereford, which improved matters. However, in the mid-19th century, bow-hauliers were still pulling craft over shallows. Charles Hadfield noted an occurrence just above Brockweir, in 1847, when a barge was moved by a gang of 32 men, working in teams of eight. Wearing chest harnesses, attached to a rope, the labour was so great that, at times, they had to get down on their hands and feet to try to get a hold.

Decline in trade on the river came about with the arrival of the railways. The Hereford, Ross and Gloucester Railway, which was opened in 1855, brought navigation of the river to Hereford, by trading boats, to an end. The Ross and Monmouth Railway was inaugurated in 1873 and the Wye Valley Railway from Chepstow to Monmouth was opened in 1876. After this time, some timber was still brought down the river from Brockweir and stone from the Lancaut quarries, but, by 1904, the river was said to be navigable only up to Bigsweir. However, there is still a public right of navigation on the Wye upstream to Hay-on-Wye. In 1989, this right was exercised when a Dutch barge, *Wye Invader*, was navigated upriver to Hereford.

In bygone days, besides barges and trows, coracles were also to be seen on the River Wye. William Coxe commented, 'During the navigation from Ross, we passed several small fishing craft called Truckles or Coricles, ribbed with laths or basket work, and covered with pitched canvas.' Samuel Ireland, calling the craft a 'corricle', described it as being 'about five feet and a half long and four broad. In the middle is a seat that holds one man, who sits with a paddle in one hand while he fishes with the other. His labour finished, he throws the corricle over his shoulder and retires to his home.' Coracles were used for both angling and netting. An early 19th-century traveller noted that many salmon were caught in a place about five miles upstream from Monmouth. The traveller saw two men sitting in their coracles, on the river, each holding on to one end of a net, which was around 20 yd. in length. The salmon fishers' course of action was to paddle at some speed down the river until they felt a fish in the net. Then, they would haul in the net quickly.

It has often been claimed that the Wye is the best salmon river in Great Britain. This may be because it is among the cleanest rivers in the country. A pool at the modern Llangurig Bridge is noted as the last pool upstream in which the salmon come to spawn. Taking its name from the Celtic St Curig, who founded a monastery here in the sixth century, **Llangurig** is the first village on the banks of Wye. For many years, it has been a stopping-off place for tourists, though 19th-century visitors, like Thomas Roscoe and Louisa Anne Twamley, were not very complimentary about its appearance. The settlement stands at the junction of the road from Aberystwyth and the road from Llanidloes. A new road, nine and a half miles long, was constructed in 1830. Winding along the left bank of the Wye, it connected the village with Rhayader. After the opening of the road, coaches to Aberystwyth used this route through Llangurig. In 1835, they included the *Sovereign* from Worcester, the *Prince of Wales* from Cheltenham and the *Tally-ho* from Hereford.

3 Dedicated to St Curig, Llangurig's parish church dates from the 15th century. The remains of an elaborately carved late 15th-century screen survived in the church until the 1830s. Using drawings made of the screen, before it was taken down, a new screen was made when the church was restored in 1878.

From Llangurig, the river takes a southerly direction. In *The Wye Tour* (1822), Thomas Dudley Fosbroke recorded, 'The river is pent up within close rocky banks, and the channel being steep, the whole is a succession of waterfalls. The Nannerth rocks, for nearly three miles, form a fine screen to the north bank.' A tributary, the Afon Marteg, flows into the Wye from the east. Then, both river and road make a sharp turn to the right, around the mass of the Gamallt, before making for **Rhayader**, a small market town on the east bank of the Wye. The name Rhayader or Rhaiadr Gwy, 'The Fall of the Wye', indicates a cataract. There was once a considerable waterfall here. This was before the clearing of rocks to make a wider channel for the river and the construction of a stone bridge in *c.*1780. The waterfall rushed over a rocky ledge, with great force, making a roaring sound, which could be heard from a distance. After the building of the bridge, the scene was much more tranquil.

Rhayader, however, was not tranquil during the unrest in the 19th century connected with tolls, which had to be paid at tollgates on turnpike roads. In the early 1840s, a secret society had been formed to abolish tollgates. At night, gangs of men blackened their faces and disguised themselves in women's clothes before destroying many of the tollgates. These incidents became known as the 'Rebecca Riots', as the gangs called themselves 'Rebecca and her daughters'. The name comes from Genesis, Chapter 24, verse 60, where Rebecca, having been chosen as the wife of Isaac, was blessed with the words, 'Let thy seed possess the gates of those who hate them'. Rhayader, situated on the turnpike roads leading from Worcester through New Radnor to Aberystwyth and from Builth to Llanidloes, was one of the areas where this rioting took place. Six tollgates were broken here, including the one at **Cwmdauddwr** when the Rebeccaites destroyed the wooden gate and threw the pieces into the river! Although tolls were reduced by the 1844 Turnpike Act, 'Rebecca and her daughters' still appeared in Rhayader for decades afterwards in connection with salmon poaching. Gangs of poachers would blacken their faces and go out at night to spear spawning salmon by torchlight. Often a great many salmon were taken illegally in this way.

Below Rhayader, the Afon Elan flows in on the right bank of the Wye. Louisa Anne Twamley remarked, 'The Elan is spanned near its junction with the WYE, by a slight simple wooden bridge that just stands high enough from the water, to let the bonny Welsh lasses trip over dry-shod.' The authoress commented on the beautiful scene at the

4 This view of the salmon leap below Rhayader Bridge was taken in the early years of the 20th century. A salmon ladder is still in place below the bridge. Rhayader's hump-backed bridge was superseded by a modern bridge in 1929.

confluence, noting 'the vales of both rivers are in view for some distance'. The **Elan Valley** was flooded to create reservoirs for Birmingham's water supply, the construction work taking place between 1894 and 1904. King Edward VII, accompanied by Queen Alexandra, formally opened the water supply on 21 July 1905. The reservoirs were named Caban-Coch, Careg-Ddu, Pen-y-Gareg and Craig-Coch. Claerwen Reservoir was built later, the Claerwen Dam being opened by Queen Elizabeth II in 1952. This spectacular chain of lakes and the high dams have been a great tourist attraction since their creation.

According to Thomas Dudley Fosbroke, the river and its surroundings, between Rhayader and Builth, had 'Grand scenery; lofty banks; woody vales; a rocky channel, and a rapid stream'. Samuel Lewis, in his *Topographical Dictionary of Wales* (1833), remarked that the scenery surrounding Llanwrthwl was 'strikingly diversified and in many parts highly picturesque'. Here, a modern concrete bridge crosses the Wye and the village is on the right bank of the river. Some way downstream of Llanwrthwl, the Wye flows past Doldowlod House, on the left bank. Fringed by Doldowlod Wood, this striking grey stone mansion was built c.1827 by the son of James Watt, the famous inventor and engineer. As the Doldowlod estate comprised land on both sides of the river, three suspension bridges used to cross the Wye here, but only one, Ystrad, remains in existence.

A bridge across the Wye gives the next village downstream its name. **Newbridge-on-Wye** was once renowned for its autumn horse fairs, which were held, twice a year, on 17 October and 12 November. Louisa Anne Twamley mentioned passing through this village, 'where a new bridge stands, as sponsor to the hamlet', and observed that Llysdinam Hall was 'beautifully placed among lawns and woods, with lodges and all other gentilities, very pretty to see'.

Beyond Newbridge-on-Wye, the lovely River Ithon flows into the Wye, on the left bank, a little way downstream of the modern Brynwern Bridge. The bridge over the Wye at Builth Road is the first railway bridge, still in use, to cross the river. It carries the Heart of Wales Railway line between Shrewsbury and South Wales. Before Builth Wells is reached, rapids are encountered at Penddol Rocks after which a substantial tributary, the River Irfon, joins the Wye on its right bank.

Builth Wells is also situated on the right bank of the Wye. Its Welsh name of Buallt comes from 'bu', meaning ox, and 'allt', a wooded height. The full name of the town, in Welsh, is Llanfair-ym-Muallt, the Church of Our Lady in Buallt. The 'Wells', in the anglicised name of the town, refers to the mineral springs found nearby at Park Wells and Glanne Wells. An iron suspension bridge across the Irfon, built in 1839, once gave access to Park Wells where there were saline, sulphureous and chalybeate springs. *Black's Guide to the Wye* (1904) stated that the waters were dispensed 'in a little two-storied pump room'. The upper part was reserved for clients who paid 6d., while the lower part was available for visitors paying a penny for as much mineral water

5 Glanne Wells, about three-quarters of a mile to the west of Builth, supplied waters from its chalybeate and sulphur wells. Visitors to these wells could drink the waters in a pavilion and there were also baths. The premises, however, were not as developed as those at Park Wells, although there was an adjoining residential house for visitors.

as they cared to drink. The sulphur and chalybeate waters of Glanne Wells could be drunk at a cost of 3d. per day.

A wooden motte-and-bailey castle was erected by the Normans, near the present Wye Bridge, to defend the crossing over the river. This fortification was later rebuilt in stone by Edward I between 1277 and 1282. In the last days of his struggle against Edward I, Llywelyn ap Gruffudd tried to gain admittance to the newly constructed castle, but was refused entry. For centuries, the townsfolk were labelled 'Bradwyr Buallt', the 'Traitors of Builth', because of this treachery. Not long afterwards, Llywelyn met his death near **Cilmery** at the hands of the English. His head was cut off and sent to London where it was put on display. A granite monolith, erected in 1956 at Cilmery, commemorates Llywelyn, the last native Prince of Wales.

Builth Wells has a long connection with markets for cattle and sheep. Samuel Ireland wrote:

> We happened to be there on market day, when the town was so thronged with people, that we could scarcely get through it. It resembled a fair rather than a market, and the immense crowd collected together, presented to the eye a scene in effect, similar to that of one continued mass of long blue cloaks, apparently in perpetual motion. Not a house, nor a stable but was

occupied, and it was really a matter of astonishment, that in so small a town, and on so common an occasion as that of a weekly market, such a vast concourse of people should have been assembled.

Today, people from far and near come together for events promoted by the Royal Welsh Agricultural Society. These are held on the Royal Welsh Showground, at **Llanelwedd**, on the opposite side of the river from Builth. The four-day Royal Welsh Show takes place in July, while the Royal Welsh Agricultural Winter Fair is held in December.

A short distance downriver from Builth Wells, the river makes a turn to the south just above its confluence with the Duhonw, which flows in on its right bank. Thomas Roscoe observed, 'Huge mountains on either side confine the valley as we advance. Aberedw Hill rises on the left bank; and Allt Mawr, on the right, erects its stern precipitous front huge and frowningly over the shadowed path.' The River Edw, once renowned for its trout and eels, joins the Wye on its left bank. The landscape in this locality is very grand with the impressive limestone **Aberedw Rocks** towering high above the river. It is thought, by some, that the stretch of river between Builth and Hay-on-Wye is as scenic as the reaches below Ross. Concerning **Aberedw**, Louisa Anne Twamley recorded:

> The village of Aberedwy occupies a beautiful and romantic situation between the two rivers, amidst scenery of a grand and lofty character. The Edwy is confined within a narrow gorge between high precipitous rocks, whose frowning crags overhang the abyss, threatening to crush the spectator who may have ventured beneath them. The church, which crowns the western bank of the river, forms a pleasing object in the landscape.

The Cambrian Railway line, which was previously called the Mid Wales Railway, used to run along the Wye's left bank with stations at Aberedw and Erwood. The latter station is now a craft centre. The village of **Erwood** is on the opposite bank of the river from the station. Its name is said to come from the Welsh, 'Y rhyd', meaning ford. In the past, drovers and their cattle crossed the river at the ford, here, on their way to markets in England. The Wye is now crossed by a modern bridge, which replaced a late-Victorian toll bridge with lattice girders. The next bridge downstream is the wooden-decked suspension bridge at **Llanstephan**. This is the river's only vehicular suspension bridge. A short distance downstream of this crossing is a hotel called *Llangoed Hall*. Built on the site of a previous mansion, it was formerly known as Llangoed Castle.

Further downriver, the six-arched Boughrood Bridge links the village of **Bough-rood**, on the left bank, with that of **Llyswen** on the right bank. Llyswen, or 'White Court', is thought to have been a residence of the early Welsh princes, while the name of Boughrood is said to derive from 'bach-rhyd' or 'little ford'. Before the former toll bridge was opened, in 1842, a boat and horse were in constant attendance at the ford. The *Boat Inn*, at Boughrood, is a reminder of the ferry.

The river forms a horseshoe bend, below Boughrood Bridge, then makes a broad curve to **Glasbury** and the modern Glasbury Bridge, which has been widened twice since it was erected in 1923. A number of bridges have crossed the river here. After the great flood of 1795 destroyed a seven-arched stone bridge, it was replaced by a wooden bridge. This was held up by stone piers at each end, with 13 wooden trestles between them. The wooden bridge, in turn, was superseded by a mid-19th-century structure, which had stone piers on the Breconshire side and wooden piers on the Radnorshire side. In the 1830s, Thomas Roscoe wrote, 'At Glasbury the Wye is spanned by a rude, singular bridge, partly consisting of stone and partly of wood, giving a very picturesque appearance to the village-like town; above which on a lawny hill stands Maeslough Castle.' The castellated mansion, built c.1829, is known today as Maesllwch Castle.

Glasbury Bridge carries the A438 road across the Wye. Along this road, to the south-west of the bridge, is the hostelry called the **Three Cocks**, well known, in the past, as a coaching inn and as a good place for anglers to stay. Charles Frederick Cliffe, in *The Book of South Wales, the Bristol*

6   The suspension bridge at Llanstephan was built by David Rowell & Co. Ltd of Westminster in 1922. It can be used by both pedestrians and vehicles. A sign at the end of the bridge indicates that, at the time of its erection, the moving load on the bridge was not to exceed a total weight of five tons on four wheels at a speed not exceeding four miles per hour. However, the weight of vehicles crossing the bridge, nowadays, is limited to two tons and only one can cross at a time.

Channel, Monmouthshire and the Wye (1847), noted that it was 'one of the most comfortable fisherman's inns throughout Wales'. Just over a century later, J. Allan Cash, in *The River Wye* (1952), observed, 'The rooms are low and beamed, and the whole place retains much of its ancient air.' Robert Gibbings praised the *Three Cocks*, too. He commented on the inn's comfortable beds and the fact that the staff knew 'how to cook potatoes so that they partake of the quality of flour rather than of soap'. The *Three Cocks* gave its name to the railway junction and station, which were once situated nearby. It was here that the Midland Railway line from Hereford to Brecon was joined by the Cambrian Railway.

The market town of **Hay-on-Wye**, with its backdrop of the Black Mountains, is near the border between Wales and England and at the meeting place of the shires of Radnor, Brecon and Hereford. Situated on the right bank of the Wye, it was known to the Normans as Le Haie, which indicated a hedged enclosure. A century ago, a Wye guidebook noted, 'Even now old-fashioned folk speak of "*the* Hay", sometimes of the *Welsh* Hay. In the past, the Welsh called it Tregelli, the 'town in the grove'. It is now known as Y Gelli. A Norman motte-and-bailey castle was first erected on the banks of the Wye, near St Mary's Church. The larger castle, in the town, was erected *c.*1200 by William de Breos, one of the Marcher Lords. Over the centuries, it suffered during border warfare and was ruined by Owain Glyndwr in the early 15th century.

Now, Hay Castle is the location of indoor and outdoor second-hand bookshops operated by Booth Books, which also run the world-famous bookshop at 44 Lion Street. Richard Booth established Hay as the 'Town of Books' in 1961. Today, there are 39 second-hand and antiquarian booksellers and printsellers in the locality. The annual Guardian Hay Festival of Literature, to which people come from all over the world, is held for ten days in early summer.

During past times, folk converged on Hay for its markets and fairs. In the 19th century, the market day for grain and provisions was held on Thursdays, a new market-house having been erected by William Enoch in 1833. Fairs for horses, cattle, sheep, pigs and farming produce were held on the Monday before Easter, 17 May, the second Monday in June, the Thursday before 1 July, 12 August and 10 October. Agricultural produce was sent from Hay to the Welsh mining districts, in the south, by means of horse-drawn trams on the Hay Railway. This tramway, opened on 7 May 1816, linked Hay with the Brecon & Abergavenny Canal at Watton Wharf, Brecon. It had a gauge of 3ft. 6in. and most of the trams carried between one and a half to two tons of goods. Besides coal and coke, brought up the canal to Brecon, the tramway also transported lime and limestone to Hay and the wharves along its route. The Hereford, Hay and Brecon Railway superseded the tramway in 1864.

At Hay, the river was also used for transporting goods. Grahame E. Farr, in *Chepstow Ships* (1954), recorded the particulars of a barge built in Hay by Thomas Thomas in 1807. She was a one-masted vessel of 39 tons and 57ft. 4in. in length, named *Penelope*. In 1841, Leitch Ritchie stated, 'The Wye ... is navigable to Hereford in barges from eighteen to forty tons; and sometimes in lighter boats even to the Hay, but the shoals in summer and the floods in winter frequently interrupt the navigation.' However, Samuel Lewis, in his *Topographical History of Wales*, published in 1833, indicated that the Wye, in the vicinity of Hay, was only navigable after extensive floods. At such times, timber was occasionally conveyed to Chepstow in flat-bottomed barges. T. Griffiths of Chepstow published a mid-19th-century guidebook on the Wye, which noted, 'The smaller kind of barges, denominated floats, ascend the river to this place; but on account of the destruction of the bridge in 1795, by a thaw which succeeded the long frost of that winter, the navigation is obstructed any further up.'

The Wye, at Hay, was also used by tourists. In 1892, R. Jordan, boat proprietor of Wye Bridge, Hereford, was advertising a 'Tour of the Wye' downriver from Hay with 'experienced watermen'. Prior to the trip, Jordan's boats could be sent on from Hereford to Hay, by rail, the station at Hay being near the river. A contemporary account of a journey, downriver from Hay, stated that the trip was quite safe, although some exciting rapids and shallows required care. Today, canoes and kayaks can be hired at Hay, by the day or week, for downstream trips.

Away from the river, the Herefordshire village of **Cusop**, to the south-east of the town, is now a suburb of Hay. In guidebooks of the past, Cusop was noted for the ancient yew trees in St Mary's churchyard and for the wooded Cusop Dingle with its waterfalls on the Dulas Brook. Cusop once had a castle, as did **Clyro**, just over a mile north-west of Hay, on the Radnorshire side of the river. In past times, Clyro was known for a mineral spring, which was said to cure diseases of the eyes. More recently, Clyro has come to the fore in connection with the Rev. Francis Kilvert who was curate here from 1865 to 1872. He wrote a diary, which gives a fascinating view of life in the Victorian era. The three volumes of *Kilvert's Diary* were edited by William Plomer and published between 1938 and 1940. Reprinted a number of times, the diary has become famous throughout the world.

Leitch Ritchie observed, 'Leaving Hay, the valley widens, the background softens, and the whole scene assumes the character of an English vale, where the hills each side are cultivated to the summit.' Downriver of the town, the picturesque ruins of Clifford Castle stand on a height above the right bank of the Wye at **Clifford**. The castle was built, after the Norman Conquest, by William fitz Osbern who became the Earl of Hereford. Later, the castle was the residence of the de Clifford family. Legend has it that 'Fair Rosamund', daughter of William de Clifford and mistress of Henry II, was born here. In the 15th century, the castle was damaged during border warfare between the Welsh and the English. It fell into ruins during the 17th century. A Cluniac priory, here, was suppressed at the Dissolution of the Monasteries in the reign of Henry VIII. The ancient church at Clifford may have been built, during the 13th century, by the monks of Clifford Priory. Dedicated to St Mary and built in the Norman style, the church was enlarged and altered in 1839 and thoroughly restored in 1888. An embattled western tower contains a peal of eight bells.

Below Clifford, the ancient half-timbered *Rhydspence Inn*, on the left bank of the river, is worthy of note. Near the border between Wales and England, it is just inside Herefordshire. This inn, like many others along the border, was once used by the Welsh drovers. Cattle were shod for their journeys along the rough roads to the markets of England and it is said that **Rhydspence** was one of the shoeing places

7 According to an early 19th-century writer, although Clifford Castle was 'considerably dilapidated', it nevertheless exhibited 'some majestic remains' at this time.

along the route. According to Grahame E. Farr, Rhydspence was where the 40-ton barge, *Sally*, was built *c.*1780. Her owner was Thomas Hughes, senior, of Monmouth when she was registered at Chepstow in 1805.

The toll bridge at **Whitney-on-Wye** is the next feature of interest on the river. This bridge is one of the few privately owned toll bridges in the country. There is a toll of 50p for vehicles, but no charge for pedestrians. The tramway track of the Hay Railway used to cross the Wye via the toll bridge. When the tramway was replaced by the Hereford, Hay and Brecon Railway, a new railway bridge was built just upstream of the toll bridge. Like a number of other railway bridges which once crossed the Wye, this was dismantled after the railway line closed.

From Whitney, the Wye meanders in an easterly direction, passing the villages of **Winforton**, **Willersley** and **Letton**, with Merbach Hill rising to a height of 1,043ft. on the right-hand side of the river. In this reach, there are salmon pools from which large catches of salmon have been obtained. These include the deep Lockster's Pool, situated on a bend in the river between Whitney and Clock Mills. Past Letton, the Wye makes a turn to the south flowing under the six-arched 18th-century Bredwardine

Bridge. Built near the site of a former ferry, Bredwardine Bridge is a link between the two roads from Hereford to Hay, which run along each side of the river.

Bredwardine, on the right bank of the Wye, once had a motte-and-bailey castle, which was part of a chain of castles erected to defend the border. The castle mound now marks the site of what is said to have been a strong fortress. One of Bredwardine's links with national history is through a 14th-century archbishop of Canterbury, Thomas Bredwardine, who was mentioned by Geoffrey Chaucer in *The Nun's Priest's Tale*. Samuel Ireland referred to Bredwardine as the birthplace of 'the famous Thomas Bradwardin, Archbishop of Canterbury, who from his variety of knowledge and proficiency in the abstruse branches of learning, obtained his title of Doctor Profundus'. The small Herefordshire village is also known as the last residence of the Rev. Francis Kilvert, the diarist, who became vicar of Bredwardine in 1877. Sadly, he did not serve in St Andrew's Church for very long, as he died of peritonitis, at the age of 38, on 23 September 1879. He was buried in the churchyard at Bredwardine, the cross marking his grave bearing the words, 'He being dead yet speaketh'.

Leaving Bredwardine, the river makes a loop around to Brobury Scar, a high sandstone cliff on the left bank. Here, the beech trees make a colourful display in autumn. **Moccas Court**, an 18th-century brick-built mansion, designed by Robert Adam, is a little way downstream on the right bank. A ferry used to connect both sides of the river. This was replaced by a private toll bridge, erected by the owner of

8 The Wye near Moccas Court.

Moccas Court, Sir Velters Cornewall, between 1867 and 1869. Situated downstream of the mansion, the iron bridge had three spans, which were supported by stone piers and abutments. Foot passengers were allowed to pass over the bridge free, but there was a toll for vehicles. The bridge, which connected Moccas with Monnington, is no longer in existence as it was damaged during the 1960-1 flood and was dismantled.

Monnington Walk, an avenue of trees, on the left bank of the river, is part of the Wye Valley Walk. Legend has it that the daughter of the early 15th-century Welsh leader, Owain Glyndwr, lived in **Monnington-on-Wye** and that he died here. The churchyard at St Mary's is said to be the final resting place of the great Welsh hero who fought against the English. Monnington is also known for the Monnington Falls on the Wye. In the days when barges were hauled upriver to Hay, a windlass or block and tackle had to be used to pull craft up the falls. The flat rocks, on the right, looking downstream, are dry at the summer water level. Canoeists have to take the channel on the left side of the narrow island, which has a small fall.

Further downriver, the Wye flows past the church of St Lawrence, at **Preston-on-Wye**, on the right bank, and past the village of **Byford** on the left bank. The name of the latter village shows that this was a fording place on the river. There was also a ferry here, in past times. Another ford and ferry were at **Bridge Sollers**. These were replaced by a cast-iron lattice-girder bridge, which was erected in 1896. Interestingly, Bridge Sollers had its name long before the bridge was built. The first half of the name indicates a crossing point or wharf, on the river, and is Norse in origin.

At **The Weir**, the National Trust has a riverside garden. Situated at a bend on the Wye, it is noted for its early spring flowers, particularly snowdrops and daffodils. Trees clothe the banks of the garden, which falls steeply to the river below. This peaceful location has fine views across the river to the Welsh mountains. A short distance below The Weir is the location of a Roman bridge. In the late 19th century, the pier foundations of the ancient bridge were said to be visible at low water, but nothing of it survives today. The bridge connected the Roman road, on the right bank, with the Roman station of Magna Castra, on the left bank, the site of which is at **Kenchester**. Over the centuries, a number of Roman remains have been found at Kenchester including bricks, lead pipes, mosaic tiles, pottery and coins.

Downstream, on the right bank at Ruckhall, is an earthwork of British origin, known as **Eaton Camp**. This was a large fortification with a single ditch and rampart. Further along, the church at **Breinton** is on the left bank. The National Trust owns land here where Breinton Spring gushes out from a rock near the riverbank. The 18th-century Belmont House, on the opposite bank, was once the property of the Wegg-Prosser family and is now a hotel with a golf course. Not far from the latter is Belmont Abbey, which was erected in 1856 on the Belmont estate mainly at the expense of Francis Richard Wegg-Prosser. This is a Roman Catholic abbey and monastery of the Benedictine order.

9 Hereford Cathedral and Wye Bridge, *c*.1852.

The three-mile stretch of the Wye, above **Hereford**, has been the scene of rowing activities for many years, even before the founding of the Hereford Rowing Club in 1861. Rowing regattas have been taking place in Hereford since 1859. Today, the Hereford City Regatta is held every year on Spring Bank Holiday Monday. The Hereford Rowing Club enters men's, women's and junior crews for both home events and those taking place elsewhere in the country. Some Hereford rowers have also competed in international events. The headquarters of the Rowing Club are between Hereford's Hunderton Bridge and Greyfriars Bridge.

Hunderton Bridge, a former railway bridge, was built between 1912 and 1913. This bridge replaced one constructed in the 1850s to carry the Newport, Abergavenny and Hereford Railway. Nowadays, the bridge is used by cyclists and pedestrians. A short distance downriver of Hunderton Bridge is the modern Greyfriars Bridge, built in 1966 to relieve traffic congestion on Hereford's ancient Wye Bridge. The latter stands just a little way below Greyfriars Bridge. The stone-built Wye Bridge superseded a wooden bridge, which crossed the river in medieval times. Erected in the 15th century, it is the oldest bridge on the Wye still standing though it has been repaired many times.

The view of the 14th-century pinnacled tower of Hereford Cathedral, rising beyond Wye Bridge, has been very popular, over the years, with artists, engravers and photographers. Although there was a cathedral at Hereford during the Saxon era, the present building dates from Norman times. Hereford Cathedral is famous for its Mappa Mundi, a striking medieval map of the world, drawn on vellum and depicting Jerusalem at its centre. It is also renowned for its chained library, a collection of around 1,500 books and manuscripts. Some of these date from the Saxon period. Said to be Europe's oldest music festival, the annual Three Choirs Festival takes place here every three years. The venues for the event, during the intervening years, are in Worcester and Gloucester.

In past times, the view from the top of the cathedral tower would have shown a busier river than that of today. Concerning the river trade at Hereford, Samuel Ireland remarked, 'The principal articles of navigation are timber, bark and grain, and the back carriage, is coals from Ledbrook and other places below Ross.' However, he added, 'the uncertain state of the river from its shoals and great rapidity, prevents that constant and uniform navigation which can alone support a regular and extensive trade.' At the time Samuel Ireland was compiling his *Picturesque Views on the Wye*, there was another hindrance to trade. The author commented, 'This being a remarkable dry season, barges have been laying at Hereford for upwards four months, for want of water to carry them down.'

A number of vessels were built in Hereford during the late 18th century and early 19th century. Grahame E. Farr noted the names and details of these boats in *Chepstow Ships*. Among them were *William*, a 43-ton barge, built in 1787 by Richard Lewis; *Kitty*, a 38-ton barge, built in 1801 by Thomas Maund; *Molly*, a 31-ton barge, built by John Thomas in 1814, and *Hereford*, a 54-ton sloop, built by Evan Hopkins in 1822. *Paul Pry*, a 31-ton steam barge, built by William Radford in 1827, was initially owned by the Wye Steamboat Company, but was purchased by buyers from Liverpool in 1828.

One of the trading vessels built at Hereford was the *Pomona*, a 108-ton two-masted craft known as a snow. She was built by Evan Hopkins, in 1823, and jointly owned by timber merchant, John Easton, of Hereford and mariner, James Williams, of Chepstow. *Pomona* would suggest that she was named in connection with the centuries-old Herefordshire tradition of growing apples for cider making. The city's Cider Museum holds the 19th-century books entitled *Herefordshire Pomona*, which illustrate the various types of apples and pears that were used in the production of cider and perry. At the museum, the different stages in cider making are shown. These include growing and harvesting the fruit, milling and pressing it and then fermenting the juice. By the early 20th century, there were a number of cider factories in the vicinity of Hereford, among them being that operated by H.P. Bulmer & Co. in Ryelands Street, Hereford.

According to *The Universal British Directory of Trade, Commerce and Manufacture* of 1791, cider, among other commodities, was conveyed in large quantities down the river to Bristol and other places. Trade on the river at Hereford, however, fell away with the opening of the Herefordshire & Gloucestershire Canal, in 1845, when cider, hops, timber, malt, oak-bark and other agricultural produce were sent via this route to Bristol. Within ten years, trade on the canal was taken away with the arrival of the Hereford, Ross and Gloucester Railway line, which was opened on 1 June 1855.

After the decline in trade, the Wye at Hereford was left to pleasure boating. In the late 19th century, boat builder Richard Jordan supplied boats for recreational use at Wye Bridge. He was said to be able to 'provide the tourist with anything floatable, from a small canoe to a boat capable of taking a party of twenty'. People used Jordan's craft for local boating, but longer trips could also be undertaken. The journey from Hereford to Chepstow could usually be made in three days, with an overnight stop at Ross and another at Monmouth. If time was lacking, it could be made in two days with a night spent at Symonds Yat. After a trip, the boat could be returned to Jordan's by rail.

Below Wye Bridge, the Bishop's Palace is on the left and a little further downstream is the site of Hereford Castle. The castle was built by William fitz Osbern c.1070 and served as a defence against the Welsh in the following centuries. Having once been a great fortress, by the time of the 16th-century writer, Leland, it was in a decayed condition. After the city was captured by the Parliamentarians under Colonel Birch, in 1645, the castle was dismantled and the materials were sold. Castle Green, a public space on the banks of the river, was once part of the castle site. It was first laid out with walks in the 18th century by Bishop Beauclerk, who was a grandson of Charles II and Nell Gwynne. In the centre is the Nelson Column commemorating Admiral Lord Nelson who was made a Freeman of the City of Hereford.

Adjoining Castle Green is Victoria Bridge, built to commemorate Queen Victoria's Diamond Jubilee of 1897 and used as a footpath to Bishop's Meadow and King George V Playing Field on the right bank of the river. Past this elegant suspension bridge, the river makes a loop before flowing under the Eign Railway Bridge, which is still in use. Built in 1931, this railway bridge superseded an iron bridge of 1866, which had replaced a timber bridge, built in the 1850s, to carry the Hereford, Ross and Gloucester Railway.

Downstream from Eign Railway Bridge, at a bend on the left bank of the river, is **Hampton Bishop**. The village inn, the *Bunch of Carrots*, has the same name as a nearby famous salmon pool on the Wye. In 1892, the proprietor of the inn, Charles Wheatstone, was advertising 'The Best Salmon Catch on the Hampton Water is within a stone's-throw of the House'. At this time, there were five other salmon catches on the Wye downstream between the *Bunch of Carrots* and the confluence of the Wye and its tributary, the River Lugg.

The River Lugg joins the Wye, on its left bank, near **Mordiford**. In the early 18th century, there was an attempt to make the Lugg navigable to Leominster. There may have been about nine half-locks, similar to flash locks, constructed on this river. They had a single gate, rather than two gates as in a conventional pound lock. Ronald Russell, in *Lost Canals and Waterways of Britain* (1982), noted the locations of three of these half-locks at Lugg Bridge, Longworth and Mordiford.

10 Holy Rood Church and Mordiford Bridge, 2003.

One of the two principal arches of Mordiford Bridge, over the Lugg, may date from the mid-14th century. The stone-built bridge also has seven lesser arches across its long causeway. Besides being used by another stream making for the Wye, these also take flood water. Mordiford is noted for the flood in 1811, which drowned four people and damaged property. An even older claim to renown is the legend of a dragon, which brought terror to the locality. The fearsome creature was said to have been killed by a man called Garson who hid in a cider barrel and fired an arrow at the dragon through the barrel's bunghole. A painting of the dragon used to decorate the central tower of Mordiford church, but this tower was pulled down in the early 19th century and replaced by a south-western tower with a pyramidal roof.

Below the confluence of the Wye and the Lugg is the modern Holme Lacy Bridge, erected in the 1970s to replace a Victorian toll bridge. Before the previous lattice-girder bridge was built, a ferry crossed the river to Even Pitt on the Fownhope side of the river. Holme Lacy's church, downstream of the bridge, is some distance from the village. Dedicated to St Cuthbert, it contains memorials to the Scudamore family. The mansion at **Holme Lacy** was built in the latter part of the 17th century for the Scudamore family, landowners who had had a residence in the locality for centuries. The poet, Alexander Pope, was a frequent visitor to the house and it was here that he wrote his lines on the 'Man of Ross'. In the 20th century, the mansion was used as a hospital, but now it is a hotel. Samuel Ireland thought that the house was a 'flat uninteresting building' adding, 'but comprises within its view a beautiful and picturesque prospect on the opposite side of the river, called Fownhope. The village is situated amidst a rich thicket of verdant and woody scenery, on an extensive slope rising from a rocky bank of the Wye.'

The ancient church at **Fownhope**, with its shingle spire, is dedicated to St Mary and dates from Norman times. There are a number of features of interest in this large church, including a centuries-old tympanum and a parish chest, which was carved out of a single oak tree. This village, on the left bank of the Wye, is known for its celebration of Oak Apple Day, commemorating 29 May 1660, the day when Charles II was restored to the throne. A claim to fame is through the prize-fighter, Tom Spring, champion of England in 1823 and 1824, who was born in Fownhope in the late 18th century. Tom's real name was Winter and he is said to have been the innkeeper, at one time, of the village's *Green Man Inn*.

From Fownhope, the Wye curves around to the steep wooded Capler Hill, on its left bank. Samuel Ireland described the scene in his *Picturesque Views on the River Wye*:

> A little below the next bend of the river, a range of hills called Capler hills, form a rich screen to the northern bank of the Wye. These hills are upwards of a mile and a half in length, and are principally covered with oak trees, the soil of which is a reddish cast, frequently breaks through the verdure of its plantations and gives a warm and animated tinge to the landscape.

The ancient woodland along the Wye at this location still has oak trees, while ash and lime trees grow here, too. **Capler Camp**, an oval-shaped Iron-Age fort, is at the top of the slope. This has double ramparts on its south-facing side and a single entrenchment on the northern side. An extensive view of the surrounding countryside may be obtained from this ancient fortification.

From Capler Hill, the Wye makes two great loops on its way to Ross. Within the first loop is **Ballingham** whose church is dedicated to St Dubricius. Flowing alongside Carey Wood, the Wye passes beneath the five stone-built pillars, which once supported Ballingham railway bridge. Formerly carrying the Hereford, Ross and Gloucester Railway, this was among four railway bridges crossing the river between Hereford and Ross, only one of which remains. Then, the Wye sweeps around to the village of **Hoarwithy** on its right bank. Hoarwithy's most striking feature is an Italianate church, dedicated to St Catherine. A tall bell tower, arcades, mosaic floors and a marble altar make it a unique place of worship. The church overlooks the river and the modern

Hoarwithy Bridge, which gives access to King's Caple. Previously there was an iron bridge here, built in 1876 to replace an earlier wooden structure. Before the first bridge was erected, in the 1850s, a ferry connected both sides of the river.

King's Caple is situated in the middle of a great horseshoe bend made by the Wye. At the time of the Norman Conquest, this settlement was inhabited by people who spoke Welsh as it belonged to Archenfield. This was a part of England where Welsh laws and customs prevailed. The red sandstone church of St John the Baptist, with its octagonal spire, is the focal point of King's Caple. A delightful custom is held at the church on Palm Sunday. Then, Pax cakes, stamped with the words 'Peace and Good Neighbourhood', are given out to the congregation by the vicar. The custom is said to have originated from money left for the distribution of bread and ale to the parishioners of Sellack, King's Caple and Hentland by a 15th-century vicar of Sellack and King's Caple.

Sellack is on the opposite side of the river from King's Caple. Formerly connected by a ferry, both villages are now linked by a suspension footbridge, constructed in 1895. Dedicated to St Tysilio, the church at Sellack has a western tower with a tapering spire. Over the years, the name of this saint has been given a variety of spellings. They include St Teseliachus, St Tesiliah and St Tesilig. Some parts of the church date from Norman times, but it was enlarged in 1841 causing one 19th-century writer to remark that it was 'a neat structure, somewhat novel in style'.

Past Sellack, the Wye flows in a north-easterly direction before making its second great loop towards Ross. At Strangford, there are the remains of another dismantled railway bridge, which once carried the line of the Hereford, Ross and Gloucester Railway across the river. Downriver of this former crossing is **Fawley Chapel** where there is a chapel dating from Norman times. **How Caple**, the next settlement, is situated near a bend in the river. This village is noted for the 17th-century How Caple Court and its adjacent church, dedicated to St Andrew and St Mary.

Turning to the south-west, the Wye passes the intriguingly named hamlet of **Hole-in-the-Wall**, on its left bank, before reaching Foy suspension footbridge. The latter links Hole-in-the Wall with **Foy** and the parish church of St Mary on the right bank. In the past, a ford and a ferry connected the two sides of the river. These were replaced by an iron suspension bridge, erected in 1876, by subscription, which was superseded by the present bridge, built in 1921.

Downstream of Foy, the river loops around Backney Common. The five masonry piers of Backney Bridge were left standing in the river when this bridge, built to carry the Hereford, Ross and Gloucester Railway line over the Wye, was dismantled. During the 19th century and first 60 years of the 20th century, there were no other crossings of the river, downstream of Backney Bridge, before Wilton Bridge. This changed with the construction of the modern Bridstow Bridge, carrying the A40, which now bypasses the centre of Ross-on-Wye.

11 A view of Ross from *The Wye and its Associations: A Picturesque Ramble* by Leitch Ritchie, 1841.

From Bridstow Bridge, there is a delightful view of **Ross-on-Wye** against the wooded slopes of Chase Hill, the site of an Iron-Age fort, with the adjacent ridge of Penyard extending to the east. The parish church of St Mary the Virgin dominates the scene. The 18th-century poet, Alexander Pope, wrote of the 'heav'n directed spire' of Ross church. His lines on the 'Man of Ross' refer to John Kyrle, the town's benefactor, who was involved in replacing the original inelegant spire of the church with a more tapered one. John Kyrle's name is also associated with The Prospect, a piece of land near the church, which he obtained on a 500-year lease and gave to the townsfolk for their recreation. From The Prospect is a striking view of the horseshoe bend on the River Wye.

In 1892, the *Royal Hotel* at Ross was promoted as adjoining the far-famed 'Man of Ross Prospect' and commanding extensive views of the Wye and its enchanting scenery. Flys and omnibuses met every train and the hotel advertised pleasure boats for excursions on the river. At this time, C. Hobbs, boat proprietress, of Wyeside, Ross, was advertising 'Pleasure Boats to all parts of the River Wye conducted by experienced and careful Boatmen'. This business was noted to be 'Under the patronage of His Royal Highness, the Duke of Connaught, Duke and Duchess of Teck, Prince George and Princess Victoria'. By the early years of the 20th century, the firm of Henry Dowell & Son was advertising pleasure boats at Wyeside. These boat builders were proprietors of the stern wheel launch, *Wilton Castle*. They also claimed to be 'Under Royal Patronage of the Royal family'. In the past, both the Hobbs and Dowell families were innkeepers at the *Hope and Anchor Inn* on the riverside.

Coracles were often used for fishing below the *Hope and Anchor* in bygone days. The last coracle used for fishing, in the vicinity of Ross, is thought to be that owned by William Dew in the early years of the 20th century. Besides fishing locally, Wye coracle men are said to have travelled great distances in these small craft. William Gilpin related a tale of an 'adventurous fellow', who once navigated a coracle, for a wager, as far as Lundy Island at the mouth of the Bristol Channel. The voyage took a fortnight and when he returned to the New Weir, some miles below Ross, it was said that the account of his expedition was received like a voyage round the world. On reading this story, Charles Heath thought the circumstances deserved further investigation. From a descendant of the person who made the voyage, he found out that the man's name was Luke Hughes and he lived at Wilton, near Ross, rather than downstream at the New Weir.

William Gilpin thought that the first part of the river from Ross was 'tame'. He wrote, 'The banks are low and scarcely an object attracts the eye, except the ruins of *Wilton-castle*, which appear on the left shrouded with a few trees.' Thomas Roscoe went exploring Wilton Castle, one evening, and found that a dwelling had been incorporated in the ruins. He observed:

> A house has been erected after the fashion of a modern dress-waistcoat dove-tailed into a suit of mail; and there it stands, in all the obtrusive, insolent bravado of upstart ignorance, jostling the hoary and crumbling fabric, with its pert venetian blinds and verandas; mocking its by-gone dignity with a pointed sash window, and forcing one tower to masquerade in the disguise of a thatched summer house!

At **Wilton**, the Wye passes under a late 16th-century red sandstone bridge, noted for its four-faced 18th-century sundial. There was once a wharf here, which, in the words of Charles Heath, was 'a convenient accommodation for the shipping and landing of goods sent up and down river'. Grahame E. Farr mentioned that corn factor, William Porter, of Wilton, operated a trow from Ross and Wilton to Bristol between *c*.1787 and 1801 and that a barge, the *Rival*, was built here, in 1804, by John Thomas. No doubt, *The King's Head*, at the Wilton end of the bridge, would have had plenty of custom in past times.

Some distance downstream from Wilton, there is another castle on the banks of the Wye. Concerning the castle at **Goodrich**, William Gilpin remarked:

> After sailing four miles from Ross, we came to *Goodrich-castle*; where a grand view presented itself; and we rested our oars to examine it. A reach of the river, forming a noble bay, is spread before the eye. The bank, on the right, is steep and covered with wood; beyond which a bold promontory shoots outs, crowned with a castle, rising among trees.

However, even though the author conceded the view was 'one of the grandest on the river', he added that he should not scruple to call it '*correctly picturesque*; which is seldom the character of a purely natural scene'.

12   Goodrich Castle from *Observations on the Wye* by William Gilpin, 1800.

William Gilpin made his voyage downriver before the erection of Goodrich Court, which was once on the same side of the river as Goodrich Castle. Contemporary opinions varied about the fanciful architecture of the 19th-century castellated mansion, which housed a famous collection of armour. Mr and Mrs S.C. Hall commented on 'unmeaning towers, and turrets, and pinnacles, in "styles" outrageously "mixed"'. The couple thought they were 'utterly "out of keeping" with surrounding objects, and sadly disturb the tranquillizing thought induced before we reach, and after we leave it'. The extensive collection of armour and antiquities was open for visitors to view, but Thomas Roscoe was annoyed by the way the suits of armour were displayed. He remarked on the 'dilapidated doll faces in the visors' and also on 'the numberless tickets and placards' scattered through all the public rooms, reiterating the request, '*Don't touch anything*', making visitors feel 'absolutely on trespass'.

Visitors to Goodrich Castle, travelling downriver, landed at the ferry house and walked up to the castle. Said to have been important from Roman times, the ferry crossing at Goodrich was on the road between Ross and Monmouth. Thomas Dudley Fosbroke noted, 'The Ferry-boat is guided by a rope, a custom certainly of the fourteenth century, and probably of the earliest date in narrow rivers.' According to Charles Heath, the ferry house, protected by a beautiful hanging wood, stood about twenty yards from the riverside where the horse ferry kept open the communication of the neighbourhood on both sides of the river. The author asserted, 'This passage over the stream, appears to have given name to the opposite parish, WALFORD, derived from the Saxon Wael-ford, the strong or rapid ford, which its current justly implies.' Mr and Mrs S.C. Hall were of the opinion that **Walford** implied Welsh ford. They, too, mentioned the very dangerous ford where the ancient road crossed over the Wye.

Over the centuries, a tale has been told of two lovers, Alice Birch and Charles Clifford, who had eloped and sought refuge in Royalist-held Goodrich Castle during the Civil War. When Alice's uncle, the Parliamentarian Colonel Birch, besieged the castle, the pair fled. They were drowned in the Wye when they tried to cross the river on horseback. One legend says that the ghosts of the couple, on their horse, have been seen attempting to cross the river, while another maintains that their spirits haunt the towers of the castle. Another tale, concerning Goodrich, is that of an encounter between the poet, William Wordsworth, and a little girl whose conversation about her four living and two dead siblings will live forever in his poem, *We are Seven*.

Boating parties, who had visited Goodrich Castle, rejoined their boats two fields below the ferry house at a point where the river flowed with less force. The path to the spot for re-embarkation led through Priory Farm, which before the Dissolution of the Monasteries was Flanesford Priory. Close by Priory Farm is the elegant Kerne Bridge, built as a toll bridge in 1828 and said, by some, to be among the most beautiful bridges across the Wye. On the left bank of the river, at Kerne Bridge, there was once a railway station belonging to the Ross and Monmouth Railway. A short distance downstream of the bridge and station, a railway bridge, carrying a single track, formerly crossed the river. This was pulled down after the line closed in 1964. The next bridge downriver also carried the Ross and Monmouth Railway. This is Lydbrook Junction Bridge, which still survives though nowadays it is a footbridge.

In *The Wye Tour*, Thomas Dudley Fosbroke described the landscape downstream from the remains of Flanesford Priory:

> From hence the Wye takes a bold turn, at which commences the proper introduction of its characteristic scenery, mountainous and rocky banks, here in fine undulating outlines of harmonious curves. Upon the rightside is the long steep ridge of Coppet wood, teethed at the beginning with a ledge of rude rocks, ground partly heath, partly wood: upon the left is Bishop's wood, a more gradual ascent, dotted irregularly with cottages, orchards, and patches of wood, all rising in amphitheatre above each other.

William Gilpin noted, 'The view at *Rure-dean-church* unfolds itself next; which is a scene of great grandeur … The deep umbrage of the forest of Dean occupies the front; and the spire of the church rises among the trees.'

The Wye makes a loop around Lower Lydbrook before flowing back on itself past Welsh Bicknor. Within the loop and situated on the right bank of the river is **Courtfield**, traditionally held to be the place where the infant Henry V was nursed by the Countess of Salisbury. William Coxe, however, pointed out that the house was of a much more modern date than the period of Henry V and that, in 1801, it did not contain anything recalling the memory of those times. He added that **Welsh Bicknor** church, about half a mile from Courtfield, contained a curious recumbent figure of a woman in stone, reputed to represent the countess. However, he was of the opinion that the person interred there was probably Margaret, the wife of Sir John de Montacute, second son of William, 1st Earl of Salisbury.

In days gone by, the riverside at **Lower Lydbrook** was busy with coal and timber being brought down from the Forest of Dean. William Gilpin recorded:

> At *Lidbroke* is a large wharf, where coals are shipped for Hereford and other places ... A road runs diagonally along the bank; and horses and carts appear passing to the small vessels which lie against the wharf to receive their burdens. Close behind, a rich woody hill hangs sloping over the wharf, and forms a grand back-ground to the whole. The contrast of all this business, the engines used in lading and unlading, together with the variety of the scene, produce altogether a picturesque assemblage.

Years later, Mr and Mrs S.C. Hall passed the village of Lydbrook and commented:

> Iron and tin are manufactured here, the neighbouring Forest of Dean supplying charcoal in abundance. The village skirts the river, and presents a busy and bustling scene; the smoke from tall chimneys rising above the foliage, and the boats and barges at the quay forming a picture somewhat singular and striking in this peculiarly rural district.

Downstream of Lower Lydbrook, Mr and Mrs S.C. Hall noted:

> We are now reaching the special beauties of the Wye. Directly fronting us is one of the most charming of its views from source to mouth, a tree-clad hill – nothing more. The hill is called ROSEMARY TOPPING, a pleasant name affixed to a scene of surpassing grace and beauty. Trees of various shades and character rise from the base to its topmost height, ending, apparently, in a point covered with a mass of rich foliage.

Then, the splendid curve of **Coldwell Rocks** appears on the left bank. These rise up, almost perpendicularly, from the river below, to a great height. Thomas Roscoe wrote, 'Approaching the foot of Coldwell Rocks, a most sublime and majestic scene presents itself. These grand, and in some places precipitous, limestone cliffs are overhung with richly varied tufts of oak and underwood, traversed by deep dells and gullies.' Louisa Anne Twamley recounted passing beneath 'their high and frowning precipices', which were 'alternately clothed with dense verdure, or standing up bare against the sky'. Today, the peregrine falcons, which nest on Coldwell Rocks, can be seen from Yat Rock.

When boating parties arrived at **Yat Rock**, they would disembark to climb to the summit. There were several cottages at the base of the rock, whose inhabitants would often act as guides. Mr and Mrs S.C. Hall mentioned that a draught of home-made cider could be obtained from one of these guides before the ascent. Leaving her companion sitting in one of the cottages, Louisa Anne Twamley climbed the height with a guide's wife as pilot. She had to slip and scramble 'through mud and through mire' and found the path 'very steep and fatiguing'. However, the authoress reported, 'I was well rewarded for my toils and tumbles, by the grand view spread around; with the Wye winding about below, and almost making an island of the lofty point on which I stood.' From Yat Rock, the river makes a great loop of over four miles, but it is only 600 yds. from the bottom of the rock to the site of the New Weir on the other side. Visitors, having ascended the height, would often descend by another path to meet their boats at the New Weir. The boatmen would take the boats around the meander, while their passengers were enjoying the excellent views from the top of the rock.

The great bend made by the Wye almost encloses the peninsula on which is located Huntsham Hill and Huntsham Court. In bygone days, there was both a ferry for foot passengers and a horse ferry at Huntsham. Due to the winding course of the river, Huntsham Ferry, known as Hunts-Holm Rope, was only about a mile from Goodrich Ferry by land, but seven miles by water. The ferry was replaced by a truss-girder bridge, built in Victorian times, which had a pronounced hump. This, in its turn, was superseded by a similar bridge, without such a noticeable hump, which was erected in 1982.

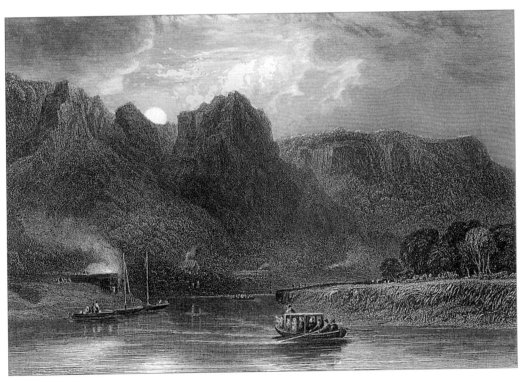

13   Coldwell Rocks from *Wanderings and Excursions in South Wales* by Thomas Roscoe, *c.*1830s.

14 Whitchurch, *c.*1900s.

Boating parties who stayed with their boats to round the peninsula would pass the village of **Whitchurch** on the right bank. Whitchurch is on the A40 between Ross and Monmouth. In past times, this was the great turnpike road from London to South Wales. The brick-built clock tower, near the centre of the village, was erected in 1867 to the memory of William Panter, John Leach Panter and their sisters by their sole surviving sister, Miss Panter. The ancient riverside church is dedicated to St Dubricius, a Welsh saint who is said to have lived at the end of the fifth century and at the beginning of the sixth. Near the church is the Amazing Hedge Puzzle, a traditional country hedge maze, which is a popular tourist attraction. This was created in 1977 to celebrate the Queen's Silver Jubilee.

Two hand-operated ferries cross the Wye at **Symonds Yat**. The first is at *Ye Olde Ferrie Inne*, on the right bank, and the second is at the *Saracen's Head*, further downstream on the left bank. During the late 19th century and early years of the 20th century, boating was a favourite pastime on the river at Symonds Yat. In 1892, William Jones was a pleasure boat proprietor, advertising 'Boats conducted personally by steady and experienced men'. Henry Williams of the Washings and Edwin Gardiner were boat proprietors in 1902, while Thomas Gardiner of Grove Cottage followed the same occupation in 1917. Today, canoes and kayaks can be hired at Symonds Yat. A 40-minute cruise may be taken aboard the *Kingfisher*, which accommodates 32 passengers, while the *Wye Pride* takes up to 50 people.

15 Samuel Ireland gave this aquatint the title 'Simmonds Rocks'. He remarked, 'Here the Wye increases in width, and its current is so strong, that it is with extraordinary labour and difficulty the barges are towed up. I have seen eight or ten men throwing themselves on the earth on every pull, to give force to their exertions.' In this view, instead of men, he drew four horses pulling a boat upstream.

Canoeists have to take care at the rapids below Symonds Yat at the site of the **New Weir**. In the 18th century, there was an iron forge here, which stood close to the waterfall of the weir. Samuel Ireland wrote of the 'awful sound of the hammers beating the fiery mass'. He described the picturesque scene as being 'much heightened by the immense volumes of sparkling smoak that are continually issuing from the forges'. The author continued:

Around the works are scattered great masses of half burned ore, coal and cinders, and interspersed on the barren and extensive moor in the vicinity, are many humble cottages of the various workmen employed in the manufactory. The roaring of the waters from the cascade of the weir adjoining to this work has a grand effect.

Concerning the setting at the New Weir, William Coxe commented:

The views at the New Weir equal in romantic beauty the scenery at Coldwell rocks; the deep vale in which the river flows, is bounded on one side by the Great Doward, a sloping hill sprinkled with lime kilns and cottages, and overhanging some iron works seated on the margin of the water; on the other rises the chain of precipices forming the side of the peninsula, which is opposite to Coldwell rocks and vies with them in ruggedness and sublimity. Near the iron works, a weir stretches transversely across the stream, over which the river, above smooth and tranquil, falls in no inconsiderable cataract, and roaring over fragments of rock, is gradually lost in the midst of impending woods.

Louisa Anne Twamley noted, 'The Great Doward is galleried and quarried from head to foot, and the smoke rising from the numerous lime-kilns scattered about, half-hiding the cottages which are perched high and low amid the cliffs and precipices, renders the scene one of great wildness and grandeur.' Coal for the limekilns on the **Great Doward** was brought from the Forest of Dean by teams of pack mules, which crossed the high ridge at Symonds Yat and descended on its south side where they were ferried across the Wye. Louisa Anne Twamley remarked, 'Many of the mules were really beautiful animals, and as they wound down the rugged and narrow path, picking their way with unerring sureness of foot, and stepped into the ferry-boat with sagacious staidness of demeanour, I heartily wished them a kindlier lot.'

William Coxe mentioned that 'a sluice was formed for the passage of boats' at the New Weir, while Charles Heath noted, 'Previous to lowering the weir, the barges trading on the Wye received great assistance from a Capstan, in towing them in and out of the Lock'. The weir and flash lock were removed in 1814. This was a help to both navigation and to salmon fishing on the river above as the weir had impeded the progress of salmon upriver.

As on other stretches of the Wye, coracles were used here for salmon fishing. Thomas Roscoe observed, 'A few coracles were on the river, with their still, patient occupants, the salmon fishers.' Besides coracles, other small boats were used on the Wye by salmon fishers. Charles Heath wrote that salmon fishing employed a number of people from the middle of November to the middle of August. He remarked, 'The method for taking them is, by mooring a boat (one end near the shore), with a net fixed to two poles: — upon the fish striking the net, the men press down the poles, which raises up the net, and secures the salmon.' The author added that the salmon fishermen were often out for more than twelve hours at a time, the greater part of which was in the night.

Writing about the Wye and its surroundings, below the New Weir, Thomas Dudley Fosbroke remarked, 'The river roars along in a curve between High-meadow woods on the left, and the rock-wall of the GREAT DOWARD on the right.' It was at a spot called The Slaughter, on the left side of the river, that a battle is said to have been fought between the Roman general, Ostorius Scapula, and the British chief, Caratacus. A narrow suspension bridge crosses the river at The Biblins. Constructed in 1957, of wood and steel mesh, it takes the Wye Valley Walk, going downstream, from the left bank of the river to the right bank.

16 Fishing punt and coracle, 1861.

Describing the stretch of the river from the New Weir, Thomas Roscoe observed:

> Lofty rocks now rise on both sides, robed in infinite varieties of wood and shrub of every imaginable tint, showing the pale grey of the limestone contrasted richly by the bright red, green, yellow and brown of the Autumn foliage. Many portions of the craggy cliffs have the appearance of ruined castles and towers.

Among these pinnacles, on the right bank, are the **Seven Sisters**, one of the renowned locations on the river. *Black's Guide to the Wye* directed visitors to look out for their 'pale maiden faces' and indicated that there were more than seven if the half sisters and baby brothers of this 'line of grand limestone crags' were taken into account. Above the latter, on the Great Doward, is King Arthur's Cave. Here, excavations in Victorian times revealed evidence of the cave's occupation by Stone-Age man and the bones of prehistoric animals such as the mammoth and the woolly rhinoceros. Below the Seven Sisters Rocks is Martin's Pool where the river is said to be at a depth of 70ft.

The **Little Doward**, a nearby height, is the site of an Iron-Age hill fort. In early Victorian times, an iron view-tower was erected here by R. Blakemore, MP, the owner of the mansion at Wyastone Leys. It was known to local folk as 'Blakemore's Folly'. Mr and Mrs S.C. Hall, in 1861, noted that the tower was 'unfinished, in consequence, it is understood, of alarm that it might attract lightning — an idea that did not occur until a large sum had been expended in its construction'. The folly no longer exists as it was pulled down in the 1920s. Wyastone Leys, in a fine position above the river, has views looking across to the Forest of Dean. At present, it is a centre for music having a recording studio and a concert hall.

Just after Wyastone Leys, the Wye makes a right-angled bend to the south and heads for **Monmouth**, passing the church at **Dixton** on its right bank. Dedicated to St Peter, this ancient church has a western tower with a low broach spire and a long nave, whitewashed on the outside. Some parts of the building date from Norman times, but most of the church was built in the 13th century. Over the centuries, it has suffered from the Wye floods. Samuel Ireland wrote, 'its interior received in the great flood in 1795 very material injury; the water having forced its way through the windows and doors, and torn up the pulpit, pews and pavement.'

Monmouth's five-arched Wye Bridge survived the 1795 flood, but the structure we see today is the result of widening both sides of the bridge in 1879. The original

17   Above Wye Bridge, Monmouth, 1861.

early 17th-century arches still exist beneath the present arches. The town is famous for another bridge, the medieval Monnow Bridge with its picturesque gatehouse. This crosses the Monnow, a tributary of the Wye. Monmouth is nearly enclosed by the rivers Wye and Monnow and its English name is derived from the latter river. In Welsh, the town is called Trefynwy.

Soon after the Norman Conquest, William fitz Osbern built a castle overlooking the Monnow. Renowned as the birthplace of the future Henry V, Monmouth Castle was in ruins by the time late 18th-century tourists were making 'The Wye Tour' as Monmouth's Great Castle House had been constructed out of stone from the castle. In 1801, William Coxe wrote that the ruins 'present an appearance of dilapidated grandeur'. Mr and Mrs S.C. Hall, 19th-century visitors, described the castle as 'a miserable and desecrated ruin', adding, 'the interior has literally been converted into a pigsty, where it is hazardous for a foot to tread'. The Great Castle House, built in 1673 by Henry Somerset, 3rd Marquess of Worcester, still stands. It is the headquarters of the Royal Monmouthshire Royal Engineers, a Senior Regiment of the Reserve Army, and houses the Regimental Museum, exhibiting the military history of the regiment and town.

Monmouth's Nelson Museum holds a fine collection of articles connected with Admiral Lord Nelson, which includes both personal items and commemorative pieces. The admiral and his friends visited the town in 1802. At this time, a public breakfast at the Kymin and a public dinner at the *Beaufort Arms* were given to the hero of the Nile by the town's corporation. The **Kymin**, high ground overlooking Monmouth, is now the property of the National Trust. A banqueting house, known as 'The Kymin Pavilion', was erected here, in 1794, by the gentlemen of Monmouth. Nearby is the Naval Temple, opened in 1801 and commemorating British admirals including Lord Nelson.

The *Beaufort Arms*, where Lord Nelson stayed, was one of the town's coaching inns in Agincourt Square. Another was the *King's Head* where Charles I is said to have slept during the Civil War. Monmouth's inhabitants must have been very thirsty, in days past, as the town boasted a great number of drinking places. Among the town's late 18th-century hostelries were the *Angel Inn*, the *Falcon Inn*, the *Cross Keys*, the *White Horse*, the *Star and Garter*, the *Golden Ball*, the *Griffin*, the *Boar's Head*, the *Globe*, the *Bull*, the *White Cross*, the *Black Swan*, the *Greyhound*, the *Bell*, the *Butcher's Arms* and the *Full Moon*. No doubt, the bow-hauliers who pulled the barges and trows upriver made full use of these establishments and of the many others in the town not mentioned here.

In centuries past, the town was renowned for the making of Monmouth caps, warm coverings for the head. Fluellen, in William Shakespeare's *Henry V*, mentioned Welshmen who were 'wearing leeks in their Monmouth caps'. Acts of Parliament were passed in the reigns of Edward IV, Henry VIII and Elizabeth I to encourage the use of caps. In the 13th year of the reign of Elizabeth I, it was enacted that they should be worn by all persons, except for some of worship and quality, on Sabbath days and

Holy Days. If they were not worn, the penalty was 10 groats. This statute was repealed during the 39th year of Elizabeth's reign. Eventually, after an outbreak of plague in Monmouth, the manufacture of caps was taken away to Bewdley in Worcestershire.

The chief trade of Monmouth, in the late 18th century, was with Bristol via the River Wye. Then, trows sailed regularly every fortnight in 'spring week' from Monmouth to Bristol and Gloucester. In 1801, William Coxe remarked:

> There are no manufactures, excepting the iron works of Partridge and company; the inhabitants are principally supported by the navigation of the Wy, the trade with Hereford and Bristol, the supply of the neighbouring districts with various kinds of shop goods, and the influx of company. Among the articles brought down the river, which give employment to many of the inhabitants, bark must not be omitted; it is conveyed in large quantities from the forests of the Upper Wy, and landed on the banks, where, after being pared and cleansed, it is sent for exportation to Chepstow.

Pigot & Co.'s National Commercial Directory of 1835 noted that weekly conveyance by water to Bristol was in barges operated by Henry Hughes, James Biss and Hezekiah Swift. By 1850, according to *Slater's National and Commercial Directory* of that year, the weekly barges to Bristol were run by Thomas Swift.

When the days of trading on the Wye were past, activity on the water at Monmouth was in the form of rowing. In the first decade of the 20th century, pleasure boats could be hired at a cost of 1s. for the first hour and 6d. thereafter. For a journey to Symonds Yat, a boat with one man could be hired for 6s. The cost to Tintern was 10s., while it was £1 to Chepstow. An additional charge was made when two boatmen were employed. Today, Canadian canoes and single kayaks can be hired by the half day, whole day or week from Monmouth Canoe Activity Centre. The Welsh Amateur Rowing Association has its training centre at Monmouth, while Monmouth Boat Club, with a boathouse and landing stage on the river, organises a summer regatta. Sadly, however, Monmouth is separated from its riverside by the A40, which runs along the right bank of the river, bypassing the town.

Downstream of the confluence of the Wye and the Monnow, two railway bridges crossed the river. The first bridge, finished in 1874, still stands. It is a truss-girder bridge with three spans, which once took the Ross and Monmouth Railway line to Troy station on the right-hand side of the Wye. Here, the line connected with another, which ran between Pontypool and Wyesham on the opposite bank of the river. The second railway bridge, constructed in 1861, crossed the Wye a little way downriver. This bridge had a lattice-girder span adjoining an approach viaduct of 20 arches. The masonry viaduct remains, but the span across the river was taken down after the closure of the line in 1964.

A short distance below the site of the second railway bridge, the little River Trothy enters the Wye on the right bank. Thomas Dudley Fosbroke observed, 'The first object just out of Monmouth, is *Troy* House, so called, because situated on the small rivulet

Trothy. It was formerly a seat of the Herberts; now of the Dukes of Beaufort, who reside during the races and assizes.'

Writing about the location of the church of **Penallt**, on the same side of the river, the author remarked:

> On the Monmouthshire side of the river, about a mile and a half below Monmouth, is the church of PENALT, situated on the side of a woody eminence, at the back of which is an extensive common. On this common is a large *oak* tree, at its foot a *stone* seat. When a corpse is brought by, on its way to the place of interment, it is deposited on this stone, and the company sing a psalm over the body.

Thomas Dudley Fosbroke, first curate and later vicar of Walford, thought that this custom was 'an evident continuation of Druidism, and Celtick customs altered into a Christian form'.

In past days, Penallt was known for the production of high-quality millstones made from the local breccia or pudding stone. Charles Heath noted, 'Very excellent mill-stones are cut in dove-tailed burrs, which millers pronounce equal to the valuable French stones; and the surrounding counties are also supplied with cider-mills from the quarries of Mr Wm. Williams of this parish.' The millstones were rolled down the hill to be despatched by the trows.

Communication between Penallt and **Redbrook**, on the opposite bank, was by a ferry, which once conveyed both horses and foot passengers over the river. The *Boat Inn* stands near this former crossing. Close by the inn is a former railway bridge, built in 1876, which once carried the Wye Valley Railway across the river. Near both ends of the bridge was a station. Penallt Halt was on the right bank, while Redbrook-on-Wye station was on the left bank. The latter was well known for its attractive flower displays.

Concerning Redbrook, Charles Heath wrote:

> The hamlet is divided, and distinguished by the names of Upper and Lower Redbrook, from standing one above the other on the bank of the Wye, part of which is situated in Monmouthshire and part in Gloucestershire, a small brook adjoining the turnpike road, that empties itself into the Wye, dividing the two counties.

The name of the settlement may have been derived from the iron-oxide colour of the water that powered the water wheels at its mills. Redbrook has had a long tradition of working in metal. An iron furnace was in Upper Redbrook in 1628, but it is probable that smelting was carried out in the vicinity in earlier times. By the late 16th century, it is said that John Coster had 26 furnaces.

Two centuries later, Samuel Ireland remarked:

> Here a considerable manufactory of iron and tin gives a new and pleasing variety to the scenery and bustle of our river. Some of the iron used here comes from Coldford, and other places in the neighbourhood of the forest of Dean, but the greater part is brought from Lancashire.

18　Constructed of iron, the single-arched Bigsweir Bridge was erected, in 1828, as a toll bridge to carry the newly built road from Monmouth to Chepstow. The latter ran from Monmouth's Wye Bridge along the Gloucestershire side of the river until it reached Bigsweir. There, it crossed over the bridge to the Monmouthshire bank. At one time, Bigsweir Bridge was the only bridge between Monmouth and Chepstow.

Metalworking at Redbrook continued into the 19th and 20th centuries, the Redbrook Tinplate Company closing in 1961.

Downriver, on the right bank, **Whitebrook** was also the scene of industrial activity, in bygone days, the brook that gave the village its name being harnessed for waterpower. Charles Heath noted, 'This place was originally settled by Germans or Swedes, who first introduced the making of WIRE into this kingdom and here practised the art. On their ruins (through the use of machinery instead of bodily labour), have been erected three valuable PAPER MILLS.' The remains of several of these mills have been transformed into residences. In past times, May Day was celebrated in the neighbourhood. Mr and Mrs S.C. Hall observed that, 'Adjacent to this village, crowning the summit of a hill, — Pen-y-fan, — still stands that time-honoured relic of Merry England, the May-pole.'

On the opposite side of the river, upstream from Bigsweir Bridge, the road to Monmouth runs between the Wye and **Offa's Dyke**. The latter is a huge earthwork, erected by the Saxon King Offa of Mercia during the eighth century. It may have been built as a defensive border between Mercia and the British to the west. Comprising a rampart, in places up to 25 ft. high, Offa's Dyke runs through the borderland between England and Wales. The earthwork can be followed, along the Offa's Dyke Path, from

Sedbury Cliffs, near Chepstow, to Treuddyn, near Wrexham in North Wales. The path runs for 117 miles from the Severn Estuary to the coast of North Wales though there are gaps in the rampart, notably in Herefordshire. The Offa's Dyke Path was opened by the Countryside Commission in 1971.

The graceful Bigsweir Bridge was at one time the only bridge between Monmouth and Chepstow. **St Briavels** is a short distance from the bridge on the left bank of the river. Situated on high ground above the Wye, St Briavels Castle dates from Norman times and now houses a Youth Hostel. Writing about an unusual custom in the village, Charles Heath remarked:

> The inhabitants of St Briavels from time immemorial to the present day, pay each of them, yearly, *Twopence*, to the Churchwardens of the parish, to buy Bread and Cheese to be distributed to such persons as shall come to that Church on Whitsunday, — and this is said to be for the liberty of taking and cutting wood in Hudknolls.

The bread and cheese used to be taken to the church in large baskets, where it was distributed immediately after the Whit Sunday service. The congregation held out their hats or aprons and the churchwardens threw the bread and cheese to them from the gallery. However, after 1816, following complaints about the undignified scramble, the bread and cheese was distributed in the churchyard. The custom still survives today. The wood initially connected with this tradition was available to the poor of the parish who cut it and made it up into small faggots. The latter were sent to Bristol, by water, where they were purchased by the bakers to heat their ovens.

Bigsweir Bridge is the upstream limit of the tidal river. Charles Frederick Cliffe wrote of 'shooting' Bigsweir Bridge, while William Coxe was 'hurried along a rapid current, called Big's Weir, where the river eddies over fragments of rock, leaving only a narrow space for the passage of boats'. Thomas Dudley Fosbroke noted the mansion at Bigsweir as being 'late the residence of General Rooke, long MP for the county of Monmouth and a descendant of Sir George Rooke, who took Gibraltar'. Louisa Anne Twamley, travelling by road up the Wye to Monmouth, commented that Bigsweir House, 'looked somewhat forlorn and forsaken, but yet had an old-fashioned stateliness in its gardens and terraces, that induced me to stay and take a long quiet survey of it, from the opposite side of the river'.

From the site of the former Big's Weir, the river winds around to the village of **Llandogo**. Charles Frederick Cliffe remarked, 'The banks of the sylvan river now becomes tidal, — mountain associations are lost, but the increasing beauty of the scenery makes amends.' Charles Heath observed:

> The river makes a fine curve, whose right screen is formed by a very extensive and lofty hill, every part of which is studded with cottages, from within a few yards of the Wye to the utmost summit of the rise. These dwellings are surrounded by abundance of the choicest of fruit trees, which produce a great quantity of cider in a favorable season, while valuable herds of fine cattle are seen grazing in the fields below.

A tourist attraction in the village was the Llandogo Falls or Cleddon Shoots, starting at the top of a steep wooded hill and rushing down to the village during rainy spells. Charles Heath remarked that it was a 'beautiful cascade', but Thomas Roscoe must have passed that way in a dry season, as he saw 'no symptoms of exhibition' at the Cleddon Shoots. In 1901, permission to view the falls, in the private grounds of The Priory, was conceded on the presentation of a visiting card.

Llandogo was once connected with the bark trade and the export of timber. Charles Heath wrote, 'Great quantities of hoops and poles, the produce of the surrounding woods, are shipped from thence to Bristol and other places.' In the 19th century, the names of the village hostelries, the *Sloop Inn* and the *Ship Inn*, denoted a link with river trade. According to *Kelly's Directory of Monmouthshire* of 1891, Alfred William, innkeeper at the *Sloop Inn*, was also a master mariner, a ship, barge and trow owner and a timber merchant. In *Chepstow Ships*, Grahame E. Farr stated that there were four boats built at Llandogo between 1812 and 1868. The barges, *Ann* and *Joseph and Mary*, were built in 1812 and 1832 by John Thomas. The trows *William and Sarah* and *Hannah Louisa* were built, by unknown builders, in 1860 and 1868, respectively.

In past times, **Brockweir** was a place where goods were transhipped for carriage both upriver and downriver. William Coxe wrote:

> Brook's Weir, a village situated on the left bank, nearly half way between Monmouth and Chepstow, exhibits the appearance of trade and activity. Numerous vessels from 80 to 90 tons were anchored near the shore, waiting for the tide, which usually flows no higher than this place. These vessels principally belong to Bristol, and ascend the river for the purpose of receiving the commodities brought from Hereford and Monmouth, in the barges of the Wy, which on account of the shoals do not draw more than five or six inches of water.

Various boats were built at Brockweir by the Swift family in the 19th century. These vessels were listed by Grahame E. Farr and included trows named *Friends* (1834 and 1844) and *William* (1837 and 1846). Larger vessels were also built here, such as the *Swift*, a brig of 143 tons (1835) and *Swift*, a barque of 310 tons (1838). A different type of craft associated with Brockweir was *La Belle Marie*, a wooden twin-screw steamboat of 31 tons, which was constructed in Gloucester. She belonged to James Dibden of Brockweir, before the First World War, and ended her days at the quayside, near Brockweir Bridge. In 1967, she was found, at the water's edge, submerged under the mud.

The lattice-girder bridge at Brockweir has three spans and was constructed in 1906. Before the bridge was built, a ferry conveyed people across the river. This ferry must have been well used when Brockweir was served by Tintern station on the opposite bank. The former station, opened in November 1876, still stands at **Tintern Parva** on the right bank of the river. The railway line closed in 1964, but Monmouthshire County Council bought the site in 1970 and the station was restored. It now houses an exhibition showing the history of the Wye Valley Railway. The railway once crossed

19 Thomas Roscoe included this view of Brockweir in his *Wanderings and Excursions in South Wales*. The author wrote, 'Brookweir or Brockweir, a prettily situated and populous little hamlet, lies on the left bank, and from the sights and sounds about I should conclude ship-building to be the reigning craft of the place; here large trows from Bristol, born up by the tide transfer their heavy ladings to lighter vessels. Brockweir is about nine miles from Monmouth, and midway between that town and Chepstow by water.'

the Wye via a lattice-girder bridge nearby, which was demolished after the closure of the line. At Tintern Parva, the ancient church stands close to the river. Dedicated to St Michael and All Angels, it was restored and partly reconstructed in 1846.

Before reaching Tintern Abbey, the river makes a loop and is crossed by another bridge. Known as the Wireworks Bridge, this connected the Tintern wireworks with the main Wye Valley Railway line on the other side of the river. Wireworks were first established up the Angidy Valley from Tintern during the reign of Elizabeth I, the Angidy Brook being used to power the water wheels. **Tintern** has a claim to fame for being the first place, in Britain, where brass was made. This happened in 1568 when German workers smelted copper with zinc to make brass. Metalworking continued at Tintern over the next three centuries.

In the late 18th century, Samuel Ireland remarked:

The neighbouring iron works belonging to Mr. Tanner of Monmouth will afford a different scene, and should be visited by every traveller ... The iron works are principally supplied from Furness in Lancashire with ore, which is dissolved by the blasts of immense bellows that are worked by means of cylinder pumps. The best qualities of the ore are separated from the dross by a water wheel and hammers, by which operation considerable quantities of pure metal are collected, and the powder is sold to glass houses. Various forges are here contrived for the purpose of forming the mutilated ore into proper sizes, from the largest bar of iron to the smallest wire.

Iron manufacture was superseded by tinplate making in the late 19th century, but this industry had declined by the beginning of the 20th century.

Tintern is famous for its Cistercian abbey. This was founded, in 1131, by Walter fitz Richard de Clare, the lord of Chepstow, and suppressed, in 1536, during the Dissolution of the Monasteries. Late 18th-century tourists, influenced by the Romantic Movement, came to the abbey attracted by its delightful situation and its ivy-covered ruins. The poet, William Wordsworth, was among the visitors, penning *Lines composed a few miles above Tintern Abbey* after his visit in 1798. Another famous visitor was the artist, J.M.W. Turner.

William Gilpin wrote, 'the noble ruin of *Tintern-abbey*, which belongs to the Duke of Beaufort ... is esteemed, with its appendages, the most beautiful and picturesque view on the river'. However, having written this, he added, 'Though the parts are beautiful, the whole is ill-shaped ... a number of gabel-ends hurt the eye with their regularity, ... a mallet judiciously used (but who durst use it) might be of service in fracturing some of them.' He commented on the 'poverty and wretchedness of the inhabitants' at Tintern Abbey, noting, 'They occupy little huts, raised among the ruins of the monastery, and seem to have no employment but begging'. Some years later, Charles Heath observed that these cottages, which were 'so offensive to the eye of Mr Gilpin', had been removed. The ivy, which once gave the ruins such a picturesque effect, was also removed, long ago, to preserve the stonework of the abbey ruins.

20   The great east window of Tintern Abbey, with its original eight lights, stone tracery and stained glass, must have been wonderful to behold, especially when the morning sunshine poured through it. This 19th-century view of the interior, drawn by H. Gastineau and engraved by W. Wallis, shows the remnants of the 'pulpitum' in the foreground. This was a screen, which divided the nave from the eastern part of the church.

High up among the rocks, on the opposite bank of the river from Tintern Abbey, is the **Devil's Pulpit**. From here, a magnificent view of the abbey may be obtained. Legend has it that, from this height, the Devil exhorted the monks of Tintern Abbey to turn away from their lives of prayer and let him be their master. There are a number of other spectacular sights between Tintern and Chepstow. Leitch Ritchie noted that the **Banagor Crags** 'form a stupendous wall of cliff, extending for a considerable distance', while William Coxe observed the **Wyndcliff** to be 'a perpendicular mass of rock, overhung with thickets'. Writing in 1801 about the view from the Wyndcliff, the latter observed:

> The summit of Wynd Cliff, which towers above the northern extremity of the grounds, commands in one point of view the whole extent of this interesting scenery. As I stood on the brow of this precipice, I looked down upon the fertile peninsula of Lancaut, surrounded with rocks and forests, contemplated the hanging woods, rich lawns and romantic cliffs of Piercefield, the castle and town of Chepstow, and traced the Wy, sweeping in the true outline of beauty, from the Banagor crags to its junction with the Severn, which spreads into an estuary and is lost in the distant ocean.

Flowing past the Banagor Crags, the Wye curves around the peninsula of Lancaut with its ruined church and passes under Piercefield Cliffs. Visitors on 'The Wye Tour' could obtain more eye-catching views from **Piercefield Park**, which stretched from near the Wyndcliff to Chepstow. William Coxe noted that Valentine Morris, one of its 18th-century owners, 'was enraptured with the romantic beauties of the scenery, carried walks through the forests, opened the finest points of view, and with exquisite

21   Chepstow from the Wyndcliff, 1841.

taste adapted his improvements to the genius of the place'. Valentine Morris was renowned for his great hospitality to visitors and the Piercefield Walks became a great attraction. Sadly, his expensive style of living, among other considerations, forced him to retire to his possessions in the West Indies where he was appointed Lieutenant Governor of St Vincent's. Having spent a considerable sum on the defence of the island, it was taken by the French and Valentine Morris, on his return to England, was imprisoned for debt.

Piercefield House and its grounds were purchased by George Smith in 1784. Sir Mark Wood became the owner in 1794 and he made considerable improvements to the place. In 1803, the estate was bought by Nathaniel Wells and it continued in his ownership for more than 50 years, while the Clay family were resident at Piercefield from the early 1860s until the 1920s. The house is now a ruin and Chepstow Racecourse, opened in 1926, occupies part of the Piercefield grounds.

The walks were still a focus for visitors in the 19th century when, according to Mr and Mrs S.C. Hall, they extended for more than three miles and were 'laid out with consummate skill, with breaks at convenient and judiciously planned openings among dense foliage'. Leitch Ritchie noted the principal viewpoints:

> 1. The Lover's Leap. 2. A seat near two beeches on the edge of the precipice. 3. The Giant's Cave, which occupies the centre of the amphitheatre and overlooks Lancaut peninsula. 4. The halfway seat under a large beech tree. 5. The double view. 6. Above Piercewood. 7. The grotto. 8. The platform. 9. The alcove.

However, Thomas Roscoe was a little disparaging about the location noting 'so much puerility of design is mixed with the grand and simple beauty of nature'. He observed, 'A group of rocks peering out from the woods skirting the river, are fancifully called the twelve Apostles and St Peter's thumb, with as little reason, or connection with their namesakes, as such things usually have.' Louisa Anne Twamley concurred with this observation, remarking, 'So far from bearing any imaginable resemblance to the human form, they reminded me of ruined towers and buttresses, being girt with copse-wood, and partially adorned with ivy.'

The sheer limestone cliff of **Wintour's Leap**, on the opposite side of the river, derives its name from the Royalist, Sir John Wintour, whose surname is sometimes spelt Wyntour. Escaping from the Parliamentarians, during the Civil War, Sir John is said to have leapt from the cliff, astride his horse. As the cliff is about 200ft high, it seems improbable that he could have survived such a feat. It has been suggested that perhaps he slid his horse down from a less perpendicular part of the height or even escaped on foot. However, the story of an escape, over the precipice, certainly makes an exciting tale, which has been handed down for generations.

In past times, another sight in this vicinity was, in the words of Thomas Roscoe, 'the broad quiet river speckled with its coracles and salmon fishers'. Louisa Anne Twamley noted:

On this part of the WYE, salmon-fishing is carried on to a great extent, and the river is sometimes spotted thickly with coracles, the primitive little boats used for the purpose. Shaped like half a walnut-shell pinched in a little in the middle, and made of wicker covered with hides or cloth prepared to exclude the water, they are light and portable; being only large enough for one person, and seem to require no small degree of dexterity in the fishermen who occupy them. They are guided and propelled by one broad paddle, but when the fisher is busy at his craft, they lie on the water so stilly, or glide so slowly down with the tide, that at first sight, no one would suspect them of containing anything living.

The right bank of the Wye, at **Chepstow**, is dominated by Chepstow Castle. Covering a large area of ground, this huge fortress was built on the limestone cliffs above the river, in an excellent position for defence. The construction of the castle was started by William fitz Osbern, in 1067, the year after the Norman Conquest. In Domesday Book, the castle was recorded as Estrighoiel though Striguil was the name by which the Normans knew it. However, the town's name stems from the Saxon 'chepe', meaning a market, and 'stow', a town. Eventually, the castle took on the name of the town.

In the past, Chepstow was also safeguarded by the Port Wall on the landward side of the town. Built in the 13th century, this 6ft. thick town wall, with its round towers, was erected in almost a semi-circle around Chepstow. Over 1,200 yd. in length and 15 ft. high, the wall curbed entry into the town. The only way into Chepstow, by land, used to be through the Town Gate where market dues were collected. Originally constructed in the 13th century, the Town Gate has undergone rebuilding over the centuries. The Town Gate and much of the Port Wall are still in existence today.

Markets were held in Chepstow for centuries, a weekly market and an annual fair having been granted, in 1294, by Roger Bigod, Earl Marshal of England and lord of the town of Chepstow. In the 1790s, the weekly market was held on Saturday and a monthly market for cattle and swine was conducted on the last Monday in every month. Very large numbers of animals, sold at these late 18th-century markets, were taken over the Old and New Passage ferries to Bristol, Bath and other destinations. In the late 19th century, the market day was still Saturday and there was a market held every fortnight, when stock was offered for sale. Fairs were held on the market days nearest 1 March and the Friday in Whitsun week. The principal fairs were the wool and pleasure fair on 22 June, the horse fair held on the Tuesday nearest to 1 August and a fair held on the Friday before 29 October, St Luke's Day.

In medieval times, Chepstow imported foreign wine and stockfish, the latter being widely used on days in the church calendar when meat was not eaten for religious reasons. According to Ivor Waters, in *About Chepstow* (1952), besides wine from Gascony, other imported goods, including honey, rosin, woad and Irish linen, were re-exported to Bristol, as Chepstow did not pay custom duty on its foreign imports at that time. By the reign of Elizabeth I, wine came into Chepstow from both France and Spain. In the late 18th century, it was imported from Oporto, while deal, hemp, flax, pitch

22 Chepstow Castle, 1801.

and tar arrived from Norway and Russia, with ships of 700 tons burthen coming into the port. At this time, great quantities of timber were sent from Chepstow to Portsmouth, Plymouth, Deptford and Woolwich for shipbuilding.

Chepstow itself had been involved in constructing ships since its early days as a port. From the late 18th to the mid-19th centuries, there were three shipyards at Chepstow. Names associated with ship building in the town include Bowsher, Hodges and Watkins, men who were also ship owners and timber merchants in the early 19th century. Concerning shipbuilding, Charles Heath observed:

> The contiguity of Chepstow to the Forest of Dean, — the large supplies of timber out of Monmouth and Herefordshires, with the very convenient Docks belonging to the merchants of this town, united with their skills in Ship-building renders the port eligible to Government for granting commissions for building ships of war, frigates, sloops, transports or victualling vessels.

Much later, in the First World War, National Shipyards were created at Chepstow and nearby Beachley. These yards were for building prefabricated ships to replace the merchant vessels which had been lost during the conflict. However, the war ended before any of the ships were launched. Afterwards, crane-building and general engineering were carried on at these works.

23 The wharf above Chepstow Bridge, 1861.

As well as providing Bristol with a number of ships, Chepstow also had considerable trade with the sea-faring city across the River Severn. In the last decade of the 18th century, there was a market boat of 70 tons burthen which sailed from Chepstow to Bristol every Tuesday, returning on Friday. The fare for passengers was 6d. and all kinds of merchandise were carried on it. By 1824, visitors from Bristol, intent on seeing the beauties of the Lower Wye, were able to arrive at Chepstow by a steam packet named the *Duke of Beaufort*. Fares were 4s. in the cabin, 3s. in the fore-cabin and 2s. on the fore deck. During the 1840s, a passenger steamer called the *Wye* plied between Bristol and Chepstow. In 1847, Charles Frederick Cliffe observed:

> The voyage by steam occupies, at the utmost, two hours. The *Wye* iron steamer starts from Bristol every morning, except Sundays, and returns in the afternoon. In the summer, the passages are always arranged, when the tide will permit, so as to enable the tourist for the day to visit the most striking scenes on the Wye between Chepstow and Monmouth.

Visitors to Chepstow in the late 18th and early 19th centuries could not have failed to notice the vibrant scene on the river. In 1797, Samuel Ireland wrote, 'Chepstow the grand and central port of the commerce of our river, is here finely displayed by the throng of trading vessels through which we passed.' William Coxe remarked that 'a singular intermixture of buildings, vessels, cliffs, water and wood is presented to view'. Leitch Ritchie noted the 'tall masts of shipping' rising from the red cliffs of the Wye as the town was approached from the New Passage.

Boats are often shown in old prints of Chepstow Castle and Chepstow Bridge or in old postcard views taken from the cast-iron bridge. Nowadays, this bridge, built in

1816, carries local traffic to Tutshill and villages on the Gloucestershire side of the river, but it was formerly on the main road into Chepstow from Gloucester and a bottleneck for traffic. The building of a new bridge, in 1987, to carry the A48 road from Gloucester, has lessened the traffic on the old bridge. By the side of the modern road bridge is the railway bridge carrying the line from Gloucester to South Wales. The last bridge on the river is just before the confluence of the Wye and the Severn. This is the Wye section of the Severn Bridge, which was opened in 1966 to carry the M4 motorway between England and South Wales. Since the opening of the Second Severn Crossing, the cable-stayed Wye section and the suspension bridge over the Severn has carried the M48 motorway.

Past writers differed in their reflections on the last reach of the Wye and its convergence with the mighty Severn. Samuel Ireland remarked that from Chepstow, 'The lofty and high impending screen of rocks, on either side of the river, rendered our passage downstream delightful. Amongst these the red rocks and Hardwick cliff are peculiarly attractive.' The author noted:

> In the latter many large apertures have been dug that are passable, and extend forty, or fifty yards from the entrance, and in the vicinity is a remarkable fine well of water, that gives the name of Thornwell, to a beautiful range of woods, adjoining the termination of Hardwick cliff.

Leitch Ritchie, at the end of the journey down the Wye, was less enthusiastic about the scenery, observing, 'From Chepstow to the confluence of the Wye with the Severn, the distance is three miles; but although the banks are in general lofty, they possess no features of interest to the descending traveller.' Mr and Mrs S.C. Hall were of the opinion that, 'The junction is by no means picturesque; it would seem as if the river had wearied of perpetual beauty, or was unwilling to grace its gigantic sister in whose embraces it was to be lost.'

Thomas Roscoe, not yet ready to relinquish the water, boarded a steamer for Bristol. He wrote:

> Proceeding steadily down the Wye, it was observable that the fair and clear mountain stream had changed to a broad and stately river. Picturesque cliffs flank her course on the left, displaying a curiously varied stratification and crowned with overhanging wood ... Gliding smoothly on, in the golden light of an Autumn afternoon, I soon found the river widening rapidly; and recognizing Aust Cliffs, and the little ruined shrine of St Tecla, on its island rock, I knew that the Wye here mingled her waves with those of her sister stream the Severn.

I have travelled countless times over the Wye and the Severn, via the Severn Bridge, and can bear witness that there is always something of interest to view whether I'm travelling from Wales into England or vice versa. There is a feeling of anticipation upon reaching the crossing and seeing the confluence of the two rivers, which both started their journeys high on the slopes of Plynlimon within such a short distance of each other, yet have taken very different routes towards their union.

PLYNLIMON

24 Samuel Ireland included this aquatint of the source of the river in his *Picturesque Views on the Wye*. Describing the scene on Plynlimon, he wrote:

> Issuing from a spacious hollow in this mountain, the water falls in a narrow streamlet several hundred yards nearly perpendicular, till meeting with various small currents, it soon presents itself in the shape of an immense cataract, rolling with astonishing rapidity over the rocky prominences which seem to impede its course.

LLANGURIG

25 Although situated at a height of over 900ft. above sea level, the historic claim that the settlement is 'the highest village in Wales' is open to dispute. Llangurig was on the intended route for the Manchester to Milford Railway, which would have joined the north-west of England with the port of Milford Haven. The bridge, in the foreground, bears witness to a scheme which never came to fruition due to lack of money.

RHAYADER

26   In *Wanderings and Excursions in South Wales*, Thomas Roscoe commented that, approaching Rhayader, the Wye was 'one continued series of rapids and cascades'. He added, 'Very, very beautiful is that wood-hung, torrent-ravine, and the more beautiful because its perpetual curves and turnings prevent the enamoured eye from grasping much of the scene at once and being satisfied —.'

27   Castle Hill and weir, *c.*1920s. A castle is said to have been built at Rhayader *c.*1177 by the Lord Rhys, Prince of Deheubarth, who was also known as Rhys ap Gruffudd. The wooden-built castle was situated on a cliff overlooking the River Wye. Later, it was probably reconstructed in stone. Rhayader Castle was devastated by Llywelyn the Great, in 1231, during his fight against the Mortimers. In the 19th century, the site of its keep was known as Tower Mount.

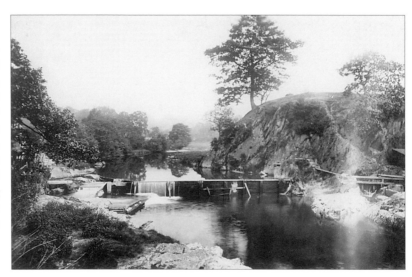

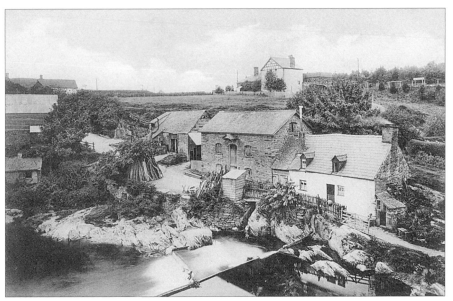

28 A corn mill was on the opposite side of the river from the castle site. Here, the salmon ladder helped the fish get upstream. The sight of salmon, enormous 'twenty pounders', leaping the weir, was termed as 'never to be forgotten' by H.L. Fletcher in *Portrait of the Wye Valley* (1968). Now, the corn mill is in ruins and the weir is no more.

29 Thomas Roscoe observed:

The Bridge, and falls of the river immediately below it, form the most picturesque scene to be found in the vicinity of Rhaiadyr. The Wye, now become a large and important stream, rushes through the one grand and lofty arch of the bridge, and, flowing rapidly onwards, is suddenly flung over a group of rugged masses of rock, forming a wide, varied and beautiful cascade.

30 In 1847, Charles Frederick Cliffe wrote about Rhayader in *The Book of South Wales, the Bristol Channel, Monmouthshire and the Wye*. He remarked, 'The scene from the bridge over the Wye, which falls from rocks into a deep black pool, is almost the only object in the town which engages the attention of a tourist, but some delightful excursions may be made in the neighbourhood.' This old postcard view shows St Bride's Church, Cwmdauddwr, from Rhayader Bridge. Originally dedicated to St Winifred, this Victorian church was erected in 1865. It replaced an earlier church here.

31 Rhayader's timber-framed market hall was at the crossroads, in the centre of the town. It had been erected by public subscription in 1762. The upper part contained rooms for the holding of courts, while underneath was an area where the market was held. *Pigot & Co.'s National Commercial Directory* of 1835 noted that the market was held on Wednesday. Around this time, there was also a smaller market, mainly for butcher's meat and other provisions, which was held on Saturday. Although much changed, the timber-framed buildings on the right of this view are still in existence. This was the location of the *Old Swan Inn*, which dated from *c.*1683.

32 This Edwardian view looks along West Street to the market hall. Even though, in the past, Rhayader was only a small town, a number of trades were carried on here. In 1906, West Street had three drapers and a clothier, besides a boot and shoe warehouse and two bootmakers. Other tradespeople included grocers, a butcher, a tailor, a milliner, a chemist and stationer, a watchmaker and cycle dealer, an ironmonger, a newsagent, a saddler and curriers and tanners. The *Lion*, 'a family & commercial hotel & posting house' was operated by Selman Solomon Fisher. John Price was at the *Cornhill Inn* and Thomas Williams was at the *Cwmdauddwr Arms*.

33 The old market hall was pulled down to make space for the war memorial, shown here at the end of West Street. Commemorating the men from the parishes of Rhayader, Abbeycwmhir, Cwmdauddwr, Llanwrthwl, Nantmel and St Harmon who fell in the First World War, the war memorial was erected in 1924. It incorporates the town clock, which was presented to the town by Mary Ann Lewis in memory of her late husband, Evan Lewis.

34 This view of North Street dates from Edwardian times. At the end of the street, the *Old Swan Inn* in West Street can be seen. On the left, in one of the whitewashed buildings, is the *Lamb and Flag Inn*. In 1906, there were two inns and a public house in North Street, plus two grocers, two drapers, a butcher, a saddler and a stationer and newsagent.

35 Church Street, looking towards West Street, *c.*1900s. The Calvinistic Methodist Hall or Bethany Chapel, on the left of this view, was erected in 1895 at a cost of £600 and had seating for 500 people. It is now known as Bethany Presbyterian Church. On the right is *Eagles Inn*, which is still in existence. In 1910, Thomas Price was its proprietor.

36 This view from Gwastedyn shows the Wye, in the foreground, making a sharp bend to the left as it starts to curve around towards Rhayader. On the right-hand bank of the bend, looking upstream, is the tannery, alongside Rhyd-hir Brook. This tannery was the last of its kind in Wales. In the past, hides from the local black cattle were used here and the bark for the tanning solution came from the oak trees, which grew on the uplands. Later, imported hides and foreign barks were employed in the tanning process. The tannery was taken down and re-erected, in 1968, in the Welsh Folk Museum at St Fagan's near Cardiff, now called the Museum of Welsh Life.

NEWBRIDGE-ON-WYE

37 Newbridge-on-Wye has been an important crossing point over the river for centuries. The Wye Bridge, pictured here c.1908, was made of wood and had six piers. It was replaced by a reinforced-concrete bridge with three spans, which was opened in 1911. This, in turn, was superseded by the present bridge, dating from 1981.

38 Newbridge-on-Wye had a population of 587 in 1901, 404 of the inhabitants being in Radnorshire and 183 being in the county of Brecon, formerly known as Brecknockshire. By the time of the 1911 census, the population had risen to 623. A variety of trades was carried on in the village during the early years of the 20th century. In 1910, there were two butchers, three grocers, a baker and a beer retailer. At this time, Newbridge-on-Wye also had two public houses, the *Golden Lion* and the *Mid Wales*, and an inn, the *New Inn*. The latter is in the far distance of this view of Crown Row on the main road through the village. There was also a temperance hotel in Crown Row.

39   A view of the main road through the village showing the Post Office, on the left, at the bottom of the slope. In 1910, the Post Office at 'Brooklyn' was run by sub-postmistress Mrs Anne Powell, who also had a boot and shoe warehouse. Later, the Post Office moved to premises on the other side of the road. The *Golden Lion* is in the background of this view, which dates from *c.*1908.

BUILTH WELLS

40 An aquatint of the river near Builth was included in Samuel Ireland's *Picturesque Views on the River Wye*. The author noted, 'From the brow of a hill about two miles before we reach the town of Builth, the scenery is peculiarly beautiful, the river spreads itself into a bay, and the immense rocky substances with which its bed has hitherto been spread, rise here in various detached forms many yards above its surface, exhibiting so many islands, and agreeable breaks in the foreground of the landscape.'

41 Leitch Ritchie observed, 'Builth is finely situated, its narrow streets rising in irregular terraces on the side of a hill on the right bank of the Wye. The houses are as Welsh as can be, and have a primitive, old world look that has great charm in our eyes.' *Slater's National and Commercial Directory* of 1858-9 noted, 'The beautiful situation of this town and its internal neatness, has induced many respectable families to make it their residence, especially in the summer season.'

42 Suspension bridge, *c.*1914. In the middle of the 19th century, Park Wells, the spa at Builth, was steadily advancing in popularity. It was within an easy walk of less than a mile and a half from the town, Joseph Bailey MP having erected a suspension footbridge across the River Irfon to shorten the distance. This bridge, built in 1839, was replaced by the present Rhosferig Bridge, which was erected in 1984 by Powys County Council.

43 Park Wells, *c.*1911. The springs at Park Wells comprised three distinct types, chalybeate, saline and sulphureous. As well as drinking the mineral waters, at the Pump Room, visitors to Park Wells could have hot and cold sulphur and saline baths, while shower and vapour baths could also be taken. In 1910, Mrs David Evans of Brecon was the proprietress.

44 Taking the waters at Park Wells, 1910. Builth Wells, in the holiday season, was a popular resort for the 'Joes and Jills of the Glamorgan collieries', as one Edwardian writer labelled them. The waters at Park Wells were bottled by the proprietor and sold to those who believed in their healing powers.

45 By the turn of the century, Builth's public recreation ground, known as The Groe, had been recently extended and a boating pavilion had been added where boats could be hired by the hour. A band played on the ground during May to October. Trees had been planted along the riverside and the pleasant pathway led to the rapids. A stretch of water, about a mile long, gave the opportunity for good boating on the River Wye at Builth. This view of The Groe and Wye Bridge was photographed *c.*1911.

47 Over the centuries, Builth has been well known for its markets for cattle and sheep. In past times, the cattle market was still held in the main street, a new market for livestock not being opened until 1910. However, even after this venue was established, the cattle and sheep still had to be herded through the town on their way to the railway station. The Edwardian shops, shown here, were in High Street. On a corner, in the background of the picture, is the shop belonging to Jenkins & Son. This was a drapers, outfitters and fancy repository. In the centre is the establishment of Gilbert Eades & Sons, boot and shoemakers. Next door, Miss Ann A. Jones sold china and earthenware goods. On the right of the picture are the premises of Barnabas Morris, ladies' hairdresser.

46 High Street, *c.*1904. Builth Pharmacy, operated by chemist, Peace Jones, is on the left of this old postcard view next to Jenkins & Son, outfitters. On the right, a clothing store has wares hanging outside the premises. Smartly dressed shoppers pose for the photographer, as do the two boys with the horse and cart and the man selling ice cream.

48 Sheep fair, Market Street. In the early years of the 20th century, market day in Builth Wells was on a Monday, but there were also a number of fairs for sheep, cattle and pigs throughout the year. These were held on 16 February, the Monday before 12 May, 27 June, the last week in August, 2 October and 6 December. If any of the fair days fell on a Sunday, the fair would take place the following Monday.

49 In 1910, the principal hotels in the town were the *Lion Hotel*, on the left of this view, and the *Crown Hotel*, further down Broad Street, on the right. Harry Colquoun ran the latter, while Henry Thomas Price was the proprietor of the *Lion Hotel*. At this time, an omnibus from the *Lion Hotel* attended the arrival and departure of every train at Builth station, on the Cambrian Railway, and the last up and down train at Builth Road station on the London & North Western Railway.

50 Thomas Roscoe included this illustration in his *Wanderings and Excursions in South Wales*. The author wrote, 'It is supposed that a bridge, leading immediately to the castle, formerly existed a few yards lower down the Wye than the present structure, which was erected in 1770, and is a long and well-looking edifice.' The six-arched stone bridge at Builth was erected jointly by the counties of Brecon and Radnor, the Wye forming the boundary between the two shires. Thomas Roscoe dated the construction of the bridge to 1770, but other authors, including Alan Crow in *Bridges on the Wye* (1995), have given 1779 as the year in which the Wye Bridge was built.

51 Looking upriver, this old postcard view of Builth Wells dates from *c*.1914. In the background is the Wye Bridge. To the right is the railway station on the Cambrian line, which ran from Brecon to Llanidloes. The River Wye separated Builth in Breconshire, on the south bank of the river, from its railway station in Radnorshire, on the north bank of the river. After the 1974 county changes, both sides were in Powys. Llanelwedd church is in the foreground of the picture.

ABEREDW

52   Aberedw is near the confluence of the River Edw with the Wye. Dedicated to St Cewydd, its ancient church has a western tower with a pyramidal roof. On one side of the churchyard is a steep precipice, at the bottom of which flows the River Edw. Thomas Roscoe remarked, 'The situation of Aberedw is most lovely; its retired village, decayed castle, and simple church, all on the banks of two rivers renowned for their scenery, form subjects for the poet's dream or the artist's study, inferior to few places in this famed track.'

53   Aberedw Rocks tower above the left bank of the Wye and extend for a considerable distance. The neighbourhood is associated with Llywelyn ap Gruffudd, the last native Prince of Wales. A cave in the area is named after him. During his conflict with Edward I, Llywelyn and a small band of men are said to have been surrounded by a superior enemy force at Aberedw. Snow was on the ground, so the prince and his followers had the shoes on their horses reversed to confuse the English. Legend has it that the blacksmith at Aberedw betrayed this strategy to Llywelyn's foes. There was further treachery when the Welsh prince was refused entry to Builth Castle. Not long afterwards, Llywelyn and his men were attacked by their enemies and the prince was killed when he received a fatal thrust from a spear.

GLASBURY

54 The drawing for the aquatint of the elegant stone Glasbury Bridge, in Samuel Ireland's *Picturesque Views on the River Wye*, was made in August 1794. The author noted, 'In the ensuing winter the bridge was totally destroyed, which will in some degree give value to this sketch, as a memorial of that which is at present, little more than a wreck; every arch of it having been blown up by the torrent of ice, which poured down on the very sudden thaw, after the long frost in the beginning of 1795.'

HAY-ON-WYE

55 Writing about Hay, in the late 18th century, Samuel Ireland observed, 'The town is happily situated on the declivity of a hill, on which the houses rising gradually, convey the idea of a place of infinitely more consequence than really it possesses, and in no small degree gives the general outline of an Italian landscape.'

56 Samuel Ireland used an aquatint of Hay Castle in his *Picturesque Views on the River Wye.* He remarked:

> The present castle stands nearly in the centre of the town. Its Gothic entrance, and the Ivy overgrowing the remains of the ancient tower, produce a striking effect on the approach to this venerable ruin. A large house adjoining is the property of Richard Wellington, Esq. It is erected on the site of the old castle, and appears to have been the work of the age of James I.

57 St Mary's Church is situated in an elevated position, overlooking the River Wye, at the western end of Hay. This engraving of the church was made before its reconstruction in 1834, which was instigated by the Rev. Humphrey Allen, the curate. Near the church, there once stood a castle built by the Normans. Even two hundred years ago, little remained other than a mound of earth and the entrenchments surrounding it.

58 The Town Clock, *c.*1910. At the top of Broad Street is the stone-built clock tower, which was erected in 1884 at a cost of over £600. Judging by the cattle in the road, this Edwardian view was taken on market day. No doubt, the *King's Head*, on the left, would have had many customers among the bystanders.

59 Market day, Broad Street, Hay. In 1910, the market was held every Thursday, mainly for provisions. The stock fair was held on the second Tuesday in every month and on the last Tuesday in August and September. By the 1920s, the weekly market was still held on a Thursday, but the stock fair was held on the last Thursday in the month.

60 Today, second-hand bookshops are a feature of Broad Street, Hay. However, when this Edwardian scene was photographed, there was a variety of tradespeople in the street. In 1910, these included an outfitter, a dressmaker, two tailors, two grocers, an auctioneer, a painter, and solicitors. There was also a coal merchant, a tanner and currier and a corn, seed, manure, hay and straw merchant. Those wishing for liquid refreshment were well served in Broad Street at this time. Situated here were the *Crown Hotel*, two public houses, the *Seven Stars* and the *Three Tuns*, and two inns, the *King's Head* and the *Black Swan*.

61 Hay Bridge, *c.*1905. At Hay, a handsome stone bridge graced the Wye in the 18th century, connecting the counties of Brecon and Radnor. This was destroyed by the flood of 1795 and replaced by a bridge, made partly of wood and partly of stone. The iron bridge, shown here, was erected on the site of the previous bridge. Completed in 1864, at a cost of between £7,000 and £8,000, it was designed by Mr W.E. Hughes of London. Tolls were levied at all three bridges. Now, a modern toll-free bridge, erected in 1957, crosses the river.

62 Hay railway station, *c.*1905. Although Hay is in Wales, its station was in England. The station formerly stood beside the Hereford, Hay and Brecon section of the Midland Railway. Hay was nearly 165 miles from London, by rail, 20 miles from Hereford and 17 miles from Brecon. In 1902, Thomas Rainbow was the station master, while Charles Williams occupied this position in 1910.

CLIFFORD

63 Clifford Castle, on a knoll overlooking the Wye, was built in Norman times to defend the ancient ford below. By the 19th century, visitors to the ruins of the castle found them, in the words of Thomas Roscoe, 'draperied with ivy and surrounded by graceful trees'.

RHYDSPENCE

64 Coming down the Wye from Wales, the *Rhydspence Inn* is the first public house in England. In existence for centuries, it was used, in the past, by Welsh drovers who were taking their cattle to the English markets. During the days when public houses were shut on Sundays in Wales, this Herefordshire inn was frequented by the thirsty Welsh from over the border in Radnorshire. In 1881, the innkeeper was Philip Clarke. John Williams was the proprietor in 1902, while the *Rhydspence Inn* was operated by Miss Ann Williams in 1917.

WHITNEY-ON-WYE

65 When Samuel Ireland passed by Whitney, in 1794, he found 'the piers and arches of a new stone bridge were in great forwardness'. He remarked, 'In the succeeding spring, the whole was swept away by that sudden thaw and torrent, whose devastations we have more than once had occasion to notice.' The present toll bridge, built in 1802, has three timber spans and two stone arches, the latter probably being part of the previous bridge. This view of the bridge dates from Edwardian times.

66 An old church, dedicated to St Peter and St Paul, once stood on the banks of the Wye at Whitney. Together with the rectory, it was washed away by floods in 1730. Ten years later, the present church, dedicated to St Paul, was built by Mr Wardour of nearby Whitney Court.

BREDWARDINE

67 The elegant brick-built bridge at Bredwardine was erected in 1769. Originally, it was a toll bridge with the toll-house on the Bredwardine bank. The toll for pedestrians was a halfpenny. One penny was charged for a horse or beast of burden, but the toll was 3d. if an animal was pulling a cart, coach or waggon. A score of calves, sheep or pigs could pass over the bridge for 5d., while the cost of the passage of a score of cattle was 10d. Four arches span the Wye and there are single flood arches on each side of the river. Fortunately, the bridge was not destroyed in the record flood of 1795, but it did require restoration after this event. By the 1920s, the old bridge was showing signs of decay. In 1922, it was rebuilt to its original plan.

68 St Andrew's Church dates from Norman times though the tower was built in 1790, replacing one that was situated further to the north of the building. The church was restored in 1875-6 when it was given a new roof. Features of interest inside include the herring-bone stonework on the north wall and the two recumbent effigies in the chancel. One of these figures may be Walter Baskerville, a lord of the manor, whose death occurred in 1369. The other is thought to be Sir Roger Vaughan, another lord of the manor, who died in 1415 at the Battle of Agincourt. The Rev. Francis Kilvert, the renowned Victorian diarist, was once vicar of Bredwardine. He is buried in the churchyard.

SUGWAS

69 This view of the *Boat Inn* dates from before the First World War, when W.L. Jones was the proprietor. The sign on the left advertises teas, which would have been very welcome to boaters rowing along the pleasant stretch upriver from Hereford. Nearby, a ferry once linked Sugwas with Eaton Bishop on the opposite bank.

HEREFORD

70 In the past, the area surrounding the city of Hereford was known for its hop-grounds and orchards. Hereford itself was and still is famous for the manufacture of cider and perry. It has also given its name to the well-known breed of red-with-white-face Hereford cattle.

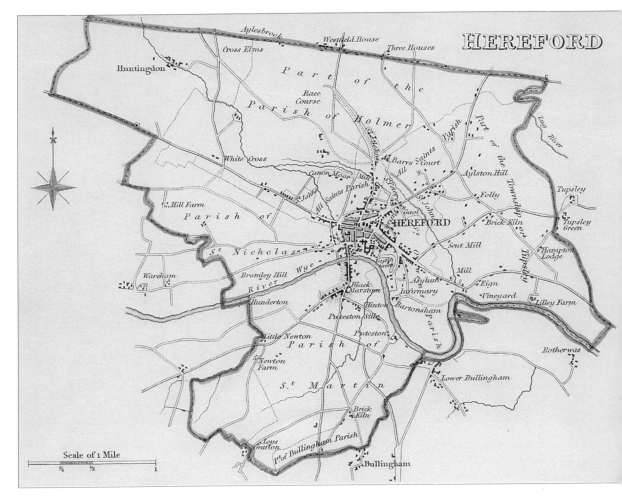

71 Map of Hereford from *View of the Representative History of England*, published by Samuel Lewis in 1835.

72 Hereford Cathedral once had a leaded spire, rising from its central tower, at a height of 245 ft. above the ground. It was removed when the western tower fell in 1786, demolishing the west front and two bays of the nave. This view dates from 1784.

73 House of the Black Friars, 1784. The ruins of the 13th-century monastery and the red sandstone preaching cross, used as an open-air pulpit by its Dominican friars, are in the grounds of Coningsby Hospital in Widemarsh Street. After the Dissolution of the Monasteries, the premises were bought by the Coningsbys of nearby Hampton Court and the stone was used for the erection of the almshouses in 1614.

74 The Market Hall or Butter Market, with its clock tower, is prominent in this view of High Town, dating from c.1915. To the left of the market, at No. 8, was Mason's, bootmakers. To the right, at No. 9, was the shop of Clarkson & Stewart, grocers. Next to the latter, at No. 10, were ironmongers Daffern & Edwards. Bootmakers, Cash & Co. carried on their business at No. 11, while another bootmaker, George Oliver, had premises on the opposite side of the street. On the east side of the street, in the background of the view, the London City and Midland Bank was at No. 35. Walter Marchant, the chemist, was at No. 36 and more bootmakers, Briggs & Co., were at No. 37.

75 Horse-drawn traffic was the norm when this photograph of High Town was taken in the early years of the 20th century. The solitary motor vehicle, on the left, belonged to Gurneys, the grocers, who had premises at No. 12 on the north side of High Town. In the centre of the view is the cabbies' hut. The timber-framed Old House and St Peter's Church are in the background.

76 The Old House was erected in *c.*1621 by John Abel. It was part of the Butchers' Row and served as the guild house of the butchers. A section of the Butchers' Row, in the centre of High Town, was pulled down in 1818 and the remainder, except for the Old House, was demolished in 1837. The Old House was acquired by the Worcester Bank in 1883 and the building was restored. Later, Lloyds Bank occupied Old House. In 1928, the Old House was presented to the City of Hereford by Lloyds Bank. It is now a museum, its three floors containing 17th-century furniture, which complement the Jacobean architecture.

77   In 1909, around the time this view was taken, Hereford's Broad Street housed a number of important buildings. These included the Public Library and Museum, on the left, where James Cockcroft was librarian and curator. Further up the street, on the same side, were the Corn Exchange and the *Green Dragon Hotel*. On the opposite side of the street were the Catholic church of St Francis Xaviour and the Post Office, where Thomas Jones was postmaster.

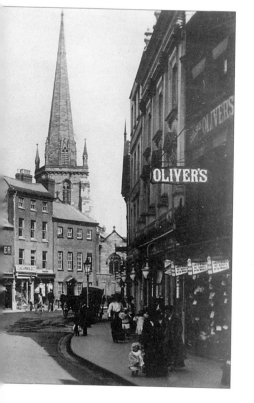

78   The *Green Dragon Hotel*, at Nos. 44 and 45 Broad Street, was managed by Miss D'Aith in 1902. Attached to it, at No. 43, was an extensive posting business, 'The Green Dragon Posting Establishment', which was operated by C. Elliott, a parcel agent to the GWR. On the opposite side of the street, the *Mitre Family and Commercial Hotel*, at Nos. 13 and 14, was run by Mrs Charlotte Almond. All Saints' Church can be seen at the end of the street.

79 In 1909, Hereford's King Street had a number of businesses, as well as shops. At the far end, near the cathedral, on the south side of the street, there were solicitors, an accountant, architects and an auctioneer at the Palace Chambers. Other businesses, on the south side, included a hotel and refreshment rooms. On the same side was the shop of fruiterer, Alfred Walter Cole. A handcart is outside the shop in this early 20th-century view.

80 The Jordan family were boat owners and boat builders at Wye Bridge. R. Jordan advertised a tour of the Wye in *Stooke's Tourist Map of the River Wye* of 1892. The tour could be taken from Hay and Hereford to Ross, Monmouth, Tintern, Chepstow and all parts of the Wye. Experienced watermen were available and boats of all descriptions were for hire, including craft for fishing and punting. At the turn of the century, the tariff for the hire of a small boat to Ross was £1, to Symonds Yat or Monmouth £1 15s., to Tintern £2 10s. and to Chepstow £2 12s. 6d. There was an extra charge of a few shillings for the daily wages of one man or more. John Jordan operated the business in the early years of the 20th century.

81 Flood on the Wye, August 1912. The summer of 1912 was one of the wettest on record all over the country. Herefordshire received a considerable amount of rain, during June to August, which resulted in the Wye flooding to a height of almost 15ft. above its summer level. This view shows Jordan's boats at Wye Bridge lying idle, while pedestrians on the bridge look at the flood waters of the swollen river.

82 Victoria Bridge, downstream of Wye Bridge, was erected in commemoration of Queen Victoria's Diamond Jubilee of 1897. It was opened in 1898, superseding a ferry established some five years previously. The designer of the suspension bridge was John Parker, while Findlay & Co. of Motherwell manufactured the ironwork. This view of the striking Victoria Bridge dates from *c*.1912.

83 The Hereford General Hospital charity was founded by the Rev. Dr Talbot, in 1776, with a £500 benefaction, while Dr Harris gave £5,000 to the building. A bequest of 1831, from Mr John Morris, led to two new wings being added. Improvements to the building were carried out in 1868 and, in the last decade of the 19th century, there were further improvements and extensions to the building. At the turn of the century, the hospital was supported by annual subscriptions and donations. In 1902, the average number of patients admitted to the hospital was around 650, while 2,500 out-patients were given free advice and medicine. This photograph of the hospital dates from *c.*1907.

FOWNHOPE

84 Situated on the eastern bank of the Wye, Fownhope once had five inns. One of these was the *Green Man*, on the left of this village view. In 1892, the proprietress was E.F. Connop, who advertised comfortable accommodation for anglers within a quarter of a mile of the River Wye and two and a half miles from Holme Lacy railway station. By 1902, the landlady was Miss Harriet Samuel. Edward Robert Samuel was innkeeper at the *Green Man* in 1909.

85 In the early 1900s, a variety of trades was carried on at Fownhope. Mrs E. West, at The Store, was grocer, baker and corn dealer. Butcher, James Huff, was at Walworth House. Charles Henry Rowberry of Manchester House was grocer, draper, boot and shoe dealer. He was also a coal and coke merchant. John Bailey was both wheelwright and blacksmith, while William Bown, at Even Pitt, was a saddler. William Henry Halford was sub-postmaster and shopkeeper at the Post Office. He was also a farmer. There were at least 12 other farmers in the neighbourhood, the main crops being wheat, barley, beans, fruit and some hops.

HOARWITHY

86 Hoarwithy Bridge, *c.*1905. Residents of Hoarwithy could gain access to King's Caple, on the other side of the river, by this iron bridge, which was almost 330ft. long. It consisted of two iron girders, crossing the Wye in three spans. Originally, the Victorian bridge had been a toll bridge, but the tolls were abolished in the 1930s.

87 Church and river, *c.*1920s. Hoarwithy's red sandstone chapel of ease, built in the Byzantine style, is an unusual and very noticeable feature in the Herefordshire landscape. Consisting of apsidal chancel, nave, cloisters on the south and a high tower, it was designed by architect, J.P. Seddon, and erected by the Rev. William Poole.

88 This view of Hoar-withy dates from *c*.1909. At this time, Williams & Mailes were grocers and bakers in the hamlet, while Andrew Mailes was butcher. Frederick Pember was blacksmith and Thomas Bond was saddler. Thomas Dance was publican at the *New Harp* and Alfred Ernest Lock was miller at the water mill.

SELLACK

89 Plans for the suspension bridge crossing the Wye from Sellack to King's Caple were drawn up by architect Ernest G. Davies, MSA, of Hereford. Replacing an old ferry, the bridge, erected in 1895, also gave Sellack access to Fawley station, two miles away, on the Hereford, Ross and Gloucester section of the Great Western Railway. The railway is now long gone, but the footbridge is still in use today. St Tysilio's Church can be seen beyond the bridge.

KING'S CAPLE

90   The church at King's Caple, dedicated to St John the Baptist, dates from the 13th century. The main part of its tower was erected in the early 14th century, but the top stage and embattled parapet were late 14th-century additions. It is thought that the spire dates from around the same time or maybe a little later. In the churchyard is a cross, known as the Plague Cross. This name possibly stems from the time of the Black Death, in 1348, as the cross would already have been in existence before that devastation. The discovery of a plague pit, near the cross, indicates why the latter kept this name over the centuries. The churchyard location is interesting as it is situated on land which once formed the bailey of a Norman castle. The motte of this castle is called Castle Tump and it stands over the road from the church. In the late 19th century, there was mention of a pleasure fair held at the Castle Tump, which was perhaps a survivor of a religious festival.

ROSS-ON-WYE

91   The Wye flows past Ross in a horseshoe bend. The Rowing Club Boat House, seen in the distance on this early 20th-century view, was erected in 1904, but no longer stands, having been replaced in 1985. The wooden building had offices, a place for storing boats and a room for ladies. There was also a balcony with railings and room for socialising on the first floor. In past times, the annual Ross Regatta was held on August Bank Holiday Monday but, in recent years, it has extended over the Sunday and Monday of this holiday.

92 In 1904, small boats could be hired for 1s. 6d. per hour with an additional charge if more than one boatman was taken. From Ross the cost of a boat to Goodrich was 6s., to Symonds Yat 12s., to Monmouth 15s. and to Tintern 25s. The boat building premises of Henry Dowell & Son, at Wyeside, Ross, can be seen on the riverbank in the background of this view.

93 In the north-eastern corner of the churchyard stands a medieval cross. This was used to commemorate the victims of a plague, which struck down 315 people in 1637. They were buried in a pit dug to the west of the cross. The building with dormer windows, behind the Plague Cross, is Rudhall's Hospital, in Church Lane, which was established in the 14th century. After the Reformation, the hospice was purchased by the Rudhall family and the occupants were chosen and supported by them and by the owners of Rudhall who came after them. The house was rebuilt by William Rudhall in the late 16th century. In 1909, around the time this old postcard view was taken, the allowance for five poor men or women was 30 shillings per annum.

94 Right: in the history of Ross, the name of John Kyrle stands out as a benefactor to the town. Born in Dymock in 1637, he died at Ross in 1724. The poet Alexander Pope made John Kyrle famous as the 'Man of Ross' in these lines:

Whose Causeway parts the vale with shady rows?
Whose Seats the weary traveller repose?
Who taught that heav'n directed Spire to rise?
The 'Man of Ross', – each lisping babe replies
Behold the Market-place with poor o'erspread!
The 'Man of Ross' divides the weekly bread:
He feeds yon almshouse, neat, but void of state,
Where age and want sit smiling at the gate:
Him, portion'd maids, apprentic'd orphans bless'd,
The young who labour, and the old who rest.
Is any sick? The 'Man of Ross' relieves,
Prescribes, attends, the med'cine makes and gives.
Is there a variance? enter but his door,
Balk'd are the courts, and contest is no more.

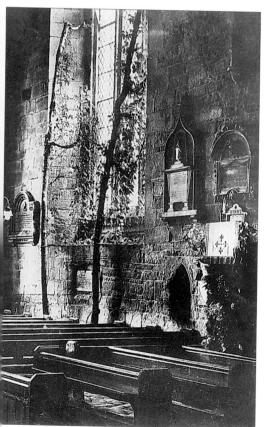

95 Left: the unusual sight of two elm trees growing inside Ross church was one of the main features of interest to visitors to the building. It was traditionally held that they were suckers from a tree planted outside the church by John Kyrle, the 'Man of Ross'. The tree had been 'impiously' cut down by a rector of the church, because it kept out the light, but the suckers found their way inside where they continued to grow to the delight of the congregation.

96 Right: Samuel Ireland used this aquatint of the Market House in his *Picturesque Views on the Wye*, but was not very complimentary about its style of architecture, calling it 'a ponderous and unmeaning heap of stone'. Thomas Dudley Fosbroke was equally scornful, dismissing the Market House as 'a building in very bad style' and noting that it probably occupied 'the site of a preceding cluster of booths and shambles'.

97 The red sandstone Market House is a focal point of Ross. Thought to date from the reign of Charles II, it is supported by pillars and topped by a small square turret. The latter, built at a later date, contains a clock with four dials. In the 19th and early 20th centuries, the upper part of the building was in use as the town hall and could accommodate 300 people. Over time, it has also functioned as a school, a place for public meetings and dances and, more recently, a library. The Market House is now used as a heritage centre. Beneath the upper chamber, stalls are still set up on market day as they were in the past.

98 This tranquil scene of the Market House and High Street dates from the first decade of the 20th century. This was a time when the traffic was so light that a horse and waggon could be left in the middle of the thoroughfare. A bust of Charles II can be seen, between the windows, above the twin arches at the east end of the Market House. A century and a half ago, the bust was described as 'time-defaced' by a 19th-century writer. It was replaced by a new bust during the mid-20th century.

99 The *George Hotel*, on the right of this view of Gloucester Road, was the nearest hotel to the railway station in 1909. Then, the proprietor was William Little and the hotel was advertised as being 'family, commercial & agricultural'. At this time, there was a motor garage and a car for hire at the garage. A meal known as a 'market ordinary' was served at 1.30 p.m. on Thursdays, which was the market day for corn, butter, cheese and vegetables. Cattle markets were held every second Thursday.

100 This view, looking down Broad Street, was photographed from the Market Place, *c.*1911. The shop of Arthur James Kiddle, tailor and breeches maker, was on the left, while Ernest S. Sacret, draper & house furnisher, was opposite at Nos. 9, 10, 11 and 12 Market Place. The premises of Innell & Wharton, wholesale and retail ironmongers, implement agents and engineers, was a little further down the road on the right. Two lamps, on the pavement outside the store, belonged to the ironmongers.

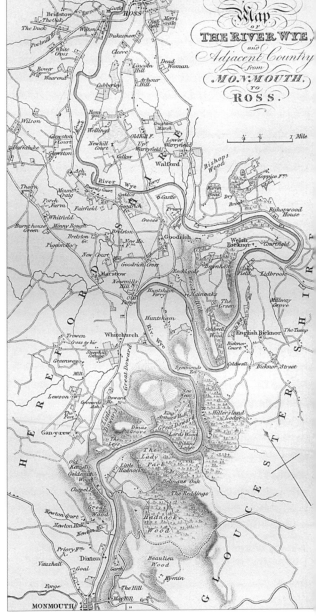

101 Above: The back of this trade card shows that the proprietor of the *King's Head Hotel* in High Street, Ross was J.J. Miles. In 1909, John James Miles operated the business. By 1917, the proprietress of *The King's Head*, a family and commercial hotel, was Mrs B. Miles.

102 Above right: In the 1830s, Thomas Roscoe wrote about his approach to the town of Ross over Wilton Bridge, 'from which a broad terrace-like road leads into Ross, only a mile distant. This new road has been recently cut beneath the red cliffs, on the summit of which the church, and its surrounding elm trees, form a conspicuous object in the landscape for some miles around.' In 1833, at the same time as Wilton Road was being constructed, the pseudo-gothic town walls and Gazebo Tower were built. The latter, originally known as Collin's Tower, is to the left of this view.

103 Right: This map of the Wye from Ross to Monmouth, dating from the 1830s, was included in Thomas Roscoe's *Wanderings and Excursions in South Wales*.

WILTON

104 Compared with other fortresses along the Wye, such as Clifford, Goodrich and Chepstow, the site of Wilton Castle is low lying. The castle, near the ford across the Wye, is said to have been erected soon after the Norman Conquest. This aquatint of Wilton Castle is taken from *Observations on the River Wye* by William Gilpin.

105 The six-arched red sandstone bridge, spanning the Wye at Wilton, was built towards the end of the reign of Elizabeth I. It suffered damage in the Civil War and during the great flood of 1795, but survived. In the past, Wilton Bridge linked Hereford and South Wales with the road which went through Ross and onwards to Gloucester and London. Today, Ross is bypassed and traffic using the M50 and A40 crosses the Wye via the modern Bristow Bridge.

106 The early 18th-century sundial on Wilton Bridge was erected by Jonathan Barrow of Bridstow in *c.*1712. However, it is no longer in the central recess on the upstream side of the bridge as in this view, which dates from *c.*1912. The sundial was moved to the opposite side of the bridge after the latter was widened in 1939. The inscription on the sundial has eroded over time. It once read:

> Esteem thy precious time
> Which pass so swift away
> Prepare then for eternity
> And do not make delay.

GOODRICH

107 Many visitors on 'The Wye Tour' would have been impressed by the views, from the river, of the turreted Goodrich Court and ancient Goodrich Castle. Thomas Roscoe wrote of 'the extreme beauty of the spot on which the Court is erected' and of the 'hoary and shattered but beautiful ruins of the old Castle of Goodrich'. Mr and Mrs S.C. Hall observed that the site was fine but that Goodrich Court was a 'blot on the landscape'. The castellated mansion had been erected in 1829, by Sir Samuel Rush Meyrick, under the supervision of the architect Edward Blore. It once contained the owner's unique collection of ancient arms and armour. Mr and Mrs S.C. Hall commented, 'Tourists on the Wye should certainly examine this singular and interesting assemblage, although to do so involves a troublesome walk, and the payment of a shilling, which we respectfully think might be dispensed with by the inheritor of so rich a store of instructive wealth.'

108 This 'View from Goodrich Old Court' was included in the title page of *An Autumn Ramble by the Wye* by Louisa Anne Twamley, published in 1839. A 60-acre park surrounded Goodrich Court. From its north front, an extensive view of the river and its valley could be obtained. The church in the distance is that of St Michael and All Angels at Walford on the other side of the river. This formerly had a spire, which was destroyed by lightning on 17 February 1813.

109 An aquatint from Samuel Ireland's *Picturesque Views on the Wye* showing the horse ferry at Goodrich, which gave access to Walford on the opposite bank. Legend has it that Henry Bolingbroke, the Earl of Derby, was at Goodrich Ferry when he heard the news that his son, who later became Henry V, had been born at Monmouth. It is said that the future king was so overjoyed that he gave the rights of the ferry and its income to the ferryman. A similar tale has been handed down locating Huntsham Ferry, downriver, as the place where the future Henry IV heard the glad tidings of his son's birth.

110 Parties on 'The Wye Tour' would alight from their boats at the ferry house and walk up to Goodrich Castle, a distance of about a quarter of a mile. In 1801, William Coxe recounted, 'Having breakfasted at a ferry-house at the foot of the hill on which the castle is situated, we ascended the steep sides of the acclivity, through rich groves of oak and elm, to the ruins, which on our approach reassumed their former grandeur.' The ferry was still in existence in the early years of the 20th century, but a contemporary guidebook warned that it was not open in the evening.

111 The first reference to Goodrich Castle was made in a document of 1101-2. The castle is said to have been originally owned by Godric Mappeston, after whom it was named. Later, the castle belonged, in turn, to the Pembroke, Talbot and de Grey families. During the Civil War, it was latterly held for the king and withstood a long siege before being ordered by Parliament to be 'totally disgarrisoned and slighted'. William Coxe noted, 'The first view of these ruins, which present themselves at a sudden bend in the river, crowning the summit of an eminence clothed with wood, is extremely grand and interesting; they vanish and reappear at different intervals, and as we passed under them assumed a less majestic, but a more picturesque aspect.'

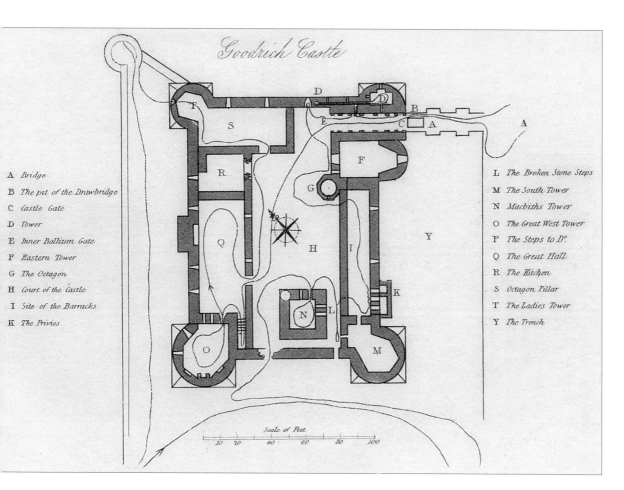

Goodrich Castle

A Bridge
B The pit of the Drawbridge
C Castle Gate
D Tower
E Inner Ballium Gate
F Eastern Tower
G The Octagon
H Court of the Castle
I Site of the Barracks
K The Privies

L The Broken Stone Steps
M The South Tower
N Macbiths Tower
O The Great West Tower
P The Steps to Do.
Q The Great Hall
R The Kitchen
S Octagon Pillar
T The Ladies Tower
Y The Trench

Scale of Feet
10   20   40   60   80   100

112 Goodrich Castle's square three-storied keep was constructed in the mid-12th century. The red sandstone curtain walls with round towers on three corners and a gatehouse on the fourth were built in the late 13th century. Louisa Anne Twamley observed, 'The entrance is very beautiful: you look under a lofty gateway, between towers canopied with ivy, along a gloomy array of portcullises and archways, extending fifty feet; then across the open area, and beyond that through a large lofty arch, which gracefully frames the picture of the distant Court.'

113 The *Hostelrie Inn* with its turrets matched the style of Goodrich Court. In 1858, Mrs Eliza Evans operated the inn, while John Charles Russell was the innkeeper by 1879. In 1902, David Williams was its proprietor and Henry Andrews ran the establishment in 1917. Goodrich Court is long gone, but the inn, now known as *Ye Hostelrie Hotel*, still stands.

114 Dedicated to St Giles, the church at Goodrich has a small square tower topped by a spire. It contains a tomb thought to be that of Sir Richard Talbot, who founded nearby Flanesford Priory in 1347 and who died in 1356. Originally, his body was laid to rest at the priory, but was removed to the church at the Dissolution of the Monasteries.

115 Samuel Ireland used a black and white sketch of the former Flanesford Priory in his *Picturesque Views on the River Wye*. He noted:

> About a mile below the castle is a small remain of Goodrich Priory; a few Gothic windows are yet standing and part of the chapel which is now converted to a granary … This priory was a monastery of the order of black canons regular of St Augustine, founded and endowed with the king's licence in the twentieth of Edward the fourth — The building with the lands contiguous to the castle are occupied by a Mr. Bellamy.

KERNE BRIDGE

116 Constructed in 1828, the five-arched Kerne Bridge was originally a toll bridge. Its tolls were abolished in the late 1940s, after Hereford County Council took over the bridge. This early 20th-century view shows its location in a very scenic part of the Wye valley. To the right of the bridge is the former Kerne Bridge railway station on the Ross and Monmouth branch of the Great Western Railway.

SYMONDS YAT & NEW WEIR

117 Yat Rocks, *c.*1905. Symonds Yat is said to derive its name partly from Robert Symonds, who was a 17th-century High Sheriff of Herefordshire, and partly from yat, the colloquial name for a gateway or pass between high ground. The Wye, unable to get through Huntsham Hill, makes a loop at Yat Rock, forming a small peninsula. From the towering height of Yat Rock, which is about 500ft. above sea level, the view is spectacular and the river can be seen on either side.

118 *Ye Olde Ferrie Inne*, at Symonds Yat West, is on the right bank of the river. In 1909, Tom Moses Davis was the landlord of the inn and proprietor of the ferry, while in 1917 the innkeeper was Henry Keddle. The hand-operated ferry at the inn still runs as does the one at the *Saracen's Head*, downstream, but only when river conditions are favourable.

119 Ferry at the *Saracen's Head*, *c.*1906. The *Saracen's Head* is on the left bank of the river at Symonds Yat East. John Jones ran this public house in 1909.

120 The railway station, being right next to the river at Symonds Yat, was useful for both tourists and anglers. The *Rocklea Hotel*, established in 1874, can be seen on the left of this view. In 1892, the proprietor and manager was Thomas Davis. Then, the hotel was advertised as being 'a most comfortable, quiet, and convenient centre or resting place', though its proximity to the railway station might have meant that it was not a tranquil retreat all the time! There were 'thirty well-appointed Apartments' and a 'pure and abundant supply of running Spring Water'. An added convenience was that visitors' boats were moored and taken care of free of charge.

121 Symonds Yat station was on the Ross and Monmouth Railway, which opened for passengers in 1873. *Black's Guide to the Wye* of 1904 noted 'the peculiarity of this station' was that it could not be approached closely by wheeled vehicles and 'boats here take the place of carriages at other resorts'. The guidebook warned that as soon as a visitor alighted from a train he would be hailed 'by the mob of shirt-sleeved gondoliers'. Other individuals, with an eye to profit and carrying refreshments, would be waiting to pounce on visitors. Passenger traffic finished in 1959, but goods trains continued to travel along the line until its closure in 1964. This view of the station dates from *c.*1904.

122 This aquatint of New Weir appeared in William Gilpin's *Observations on the River Wye*. The author noted:

> The river is wider than usual in this part; and takes a sweep around a towering promontory of rock; which forms the side-screen on the left, and is the grand feature of the view ... Near the top a pointed fragment of solitary rock, rising above the rest, has rather fantastic appearance; but it is not without its effect in marking the scene ... On the right side of the Wye, opposite the rock we have just described, the bank forms a woody amphitheatre, following the course of the stream, round the promontory. Its lower skirts are adorned with a hamlet; in the midst of which, volumes of thick smoke, thrown up at intervals from an iron-forge as its fires receive fresh fuel, add double grandeur to the scene.

123 Leitch Ritchie included this engraving of the New Weir in his book *The Wye and its Associations: A Picturesque Ramble*. William Gilpin described the scene:

> The whole river at this place makes a precipitate fall; of no great height indeed, but enough to merit the name of a cascade, though to the eye, above the stream, it is an object of no consequence. In all the scenes we had yet passed, the water moving with a slow and solemn pace, the objects around kept time, as it were, with it; and every steep, and every rock which hung over the river, was awful, tranquil and majestic. But here the violence of the stream, and the roaring of the waters impressed a new character on the scene: all was agitation and uproar; and every steep and every rock stared with wildness and terror.

124 A view looking upstream taken from Thomas Roscoe's *Wanderings and Excursions in South Wales*. The author observed, 'The New Weir here received our boat in its swelling eddy, and the foaming, roaring water added not a little to the interest of the scene.' He included William Gilpin's description of the setting in his book, adding:

> Now, however, all is tranquil, save the noise of the rapid current over the river where the Weir was erected – the works are pulled down and the population gone. To view the scene to the best advantage, the tourist should descend from the summit of Symond's Yat by the winding road traversed by the mules which brought coal from the forest when the works were used.

THE SEVEN SISTERS

125 The bare limestone crags, known as the Seven Sisters, show through the surrounding woodland cover. Louisa Anne Twamley commented:

> The Great Doward now brings its giant form into our landscape, and its fantastic cliffs of grey limestone wear the most striking and singular shapes imaginable — towers, turrets, buttresses, and bastions rise behind and above one another, and the changes they perpetually assume, as the boat varies the point of view, are as beautiful, as they are strange and novel.

DIXTON

126 Concerning Dixton, Charles Heath remarked:

> A short distance below Hadnock, on the opposite side of the Wye, stands the neat church of that name; which makes no figure as a picturesque object, viewed from the river, by reason of its awkward form, being long and narrow, — measuring from east to west about forty yards in its utmost extent, — and its spire (or rather want of it), gives the whole a heavy appearance. The parish is divided by the river, and called 'Dixton Newton', and 'Dixton Hadnock', from its respective shore.

MONMOUTH

127 Describing the approach to Monmouth by river, Charles Heath wrote, 'From Hadnock, thro' a beautiful *Reach*, 2 miles in extent, with great hanging woods, on the right or left bank, near the whole of the way (ornamented, in the perspective, by the beautiful SPIRE of the Church), we arrive at Wye Bridge.' This aquatint, from Samuel Ireland's *Picturesque Views on the River Wye*, shows Dixton church, on the right, the Wye Bridge, on the left, and St Mary's Church in the centre.

128 View of Monmouth from Thomas Roscoe's *Wanderings and Excursions in South Wales*. The author wrote, 'The approach to Monmouth is very pleasing and the town occupies a position of great beauty, lying in a valley surrounded by hills and nearly encircled by two rivers, the Wye and the Monnow.' Louisa Anne Twamley used the same engraving in her book, *An Autumn Ramble by the Wye*. The authoress stayed a long time contemplating the scene from this spot. She recalled that her visit coincided with the races, held annually in Chippenham Mead, and although she was not inclined to witness the sport, 'yet the glitter and animation given to the picture by the concourse of gay and busy people, added considerably to its beauty'.

129 Right: The original church of St Mary belonged to a Benedictine priory. This was pulled down and the church was reconstructed in 1737. Then, only the tower and the lower part of the spire remained of the ancient building. Between 1882 and 1883, the church was remodelled. The work was directed by G.E. Street and cost £7,000. The tapering spire rises to 200ft. and is a landmark in the town.

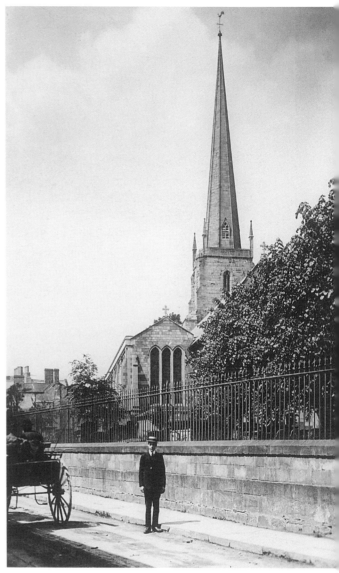

130 Left: To the north of St Mary's Church are the remains of the Benedictine priory, founded in the reign of Henry I. In one part of the building is a projecting window, traditionally called Geoffrey's Window, after Geoffrey of Monmouth, the 12th-century chronicler. However, the window is thought to be of a much later date than the time of Geoffrey, who was probably educated at the monastery. He was consecrated Bishop of St Asaph in 1152.

131 Monmouth Castle, standing on a height overlooking the River Monnow and the adjacent meadows, was once renowned as the birthplace of Henry V, who was born here on 9 August 1387. However, by the late 18th century the castle was in ruins. William Gilpin commented, 'The transmutations of time are often ludicrous. Monmouth-castle was formerly the palace of a king, and the birth-place of a mighty prince: it is now converted into a yard for fatting ducks.'

132 The focal point of Monmouth is Agincourt Square. The main streets branch out from here. Monnow Street runs downhill to Monnow Bridge across the river Monnow, while Priory Street proceeds in the opposite direction. St Mary Street leads into Wye Bridge Street, which crosses the River Wye. This early 20th-century view of the square also shows Church Street. The shop of chemist and druggist Josiah Evans was on the corner of Agincourt Square and Church Street. On the left of the picture is *Market Tavern*, which was operated by William Nettleton in 1901. The sign on the wall above the public house advertises the business of William Hughes, outfitter, who had premises at Nos. 1 & 2 Priory Street.

133 The outside of the Shire Hall, venue for the Assizes, the petty sessions and the County Court, looks busy in this old postcard view dating from the early 1920s. Situated in Agincourt Square, the Shire Hall was erected on the site of the old market house in 1724. It has an open arcaded basement and an upper storey distinguished by tall arched windows. Between the latter is a niche in which there is a statue of Henry V, the hero of Agincourt, who was born in Monmouth Castle. In the square in front of the building is a statue of the Hon. C.S. Rolls, son of Lord and Lady Llangattock, who died while flying at the Bournemouth aviation meeting on 12 July 1910.

134 Monmouth's five-arched Wye Bridge, with its huge stone piers, dates from 1617, but was widened in the late 19th century. Located close to the bridge is Monmouth School, formerly known as Monmouth Grammar School, which was founded, in 1615, by William Jones, a member of the Haberdashers' Company of London. Originally, it was a school for 100 boys, but by the early years of the 20th century the school had around 140 pupils including boarders.

135 Monmouth's High School for Girls was built in the late 1890s at a cost of £20,000. Situated in an elevated position, with south-facing views, it comprised a large hall, classrooms, music rooms and an art studio. At the turn of the century, the school was able to take 100 day pupils and 50 boarders and already had upwards of 100 scholars.

136 Monnow Street, Monmouth's chief thoroughfare, was once the venue for the town's market as it was broad and had a gate at each end. In the past, the street had a number of inns and public houses. In 1923, they included the *Fountain Inn* at No. 7, the *King's Arms* at No. 47, the *Butchers' Arms* at No. 50, the *Vine Tree* at No. 57 and the *Barley Mow* at No. 125. This view, dating from the 1920s, is looking up Monnow Street.

137 The three-arched Monnow Bridge, at the western entrance to the town, is topped by a picturesque medieval gateway, one of four town gates, which existed in the time of John Leland, the 16th-century writer. William Coxe stated, 'It commanded the passage of the Monnow, and was a barrier against the Welsh.' In fact, the gateway was primarily used as a toll-house rather than a defence.

138 This illustration of the ancient church of St Thomas and Monnow Bridge was included in *An Historical Tour in Monmouthshire* by William Coxe. Concerning the church, the author wrote, 'The simplicity of its form, the circular shape of the doorways and of the arch separating the nave from the chancel, and the style of their ornaments, which bear a Saxon character, seem to indicate that it was constructed before the conquest.' Later writers put the date of construction as the 12th century.

139 St Thomas's Square and Cross is situated near the church of St Thomas in Over Monnow. The base of the original cross was used for a new structure, erected in 1888, with three graduated steps leading up to it. Four carved figures, representing saints, were put in the recesses of the head of the cross. In this early 20th-century view, a man is sitting on the side of the horse trough, which commemorated Queen Victoria's Diamond Jubilee of 1897. On the right is the *Troy Inn*, while, in the background, the last building on the right is the *Britannia Inn*, in Drybridge Street.

140 For two centuries and more, visitors have crossed the Wye Bridge on their way to the Kymin, a hill on the left bank of the river. From the top of the hill, ten counties can be seen. They are Monmouthshire, Gloucestershire, Herefordshire, Worcestershire, Shropshire, Somerset, Breconshire, Glamorgan, Radnorshire and Montgomeryshire.

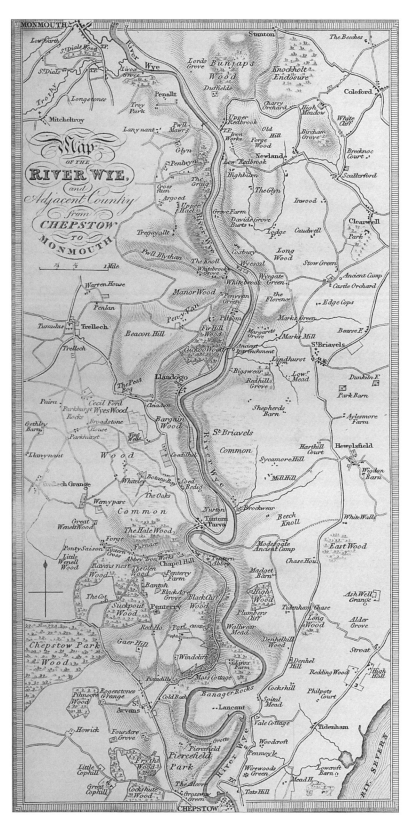

141 This map of the Wye from Monmouth to Chepstow, dating from the 1830s, is taken from Thomas Roscoe's *Wanderings and Excursions in South Wales*.

REDBROOK

142 Visitors on 'The Wye Tour' would find that, as well as scenes of unsurpassed beauty, there was also evidence of the industrial age along the river. Writing in 1861 about Redbrook, Mr and Mrs S.C. Hall noted:

> Soon we reach a very different scene, affording all the advantages of contrast; for rising above a mass of thick foliage, is the dense column of smoke that tells the whereabouts of a manufactory ... There are quays here: we note the bustle of commerce, — other life than that of the stream and the forest. The masts of many barges rise from the river: they are loading or unloading. It is the manufactory of tin — or, rather, of tin in combination with iron — that gathers a population here, and breaks, pleasantly or unpleasantly, according to the mood of the wanderer, the sameness and solitude of the banks of the Wye.

LLANDOGO

143 In 1797, Samuel Ireland wrote, 'Amidst a range of beautiful scenery we pass the pleasant village of Llandogar ... Here the river forms a smooth and glassy bay, through which the white sailed vessel is seen constantly gliding, or lying moored on the shore to take in her freight.'

144 Right: When Mr and Mrs S.C. Hall reached Llandogo, they found 'evidence of active trade' as there were boats moored at small quays on either side of the river. The trow, *William and Sarah*, was built at Llandogo in 1860. She belonged to William Williams, a barge owner of Llandogo. The village, so often associated with trows, gave its name to the famous Bristol inn, the *Llandoger Trow*.

145 Below: The trow lying on the shoal on the Gloucestershire side of the river is likely to be the *George and Mary*, which was built at Newport in 1851. Grahame E. Farr, in *Chepstow Ships*, noted that this vessel, originally of 46 tons, was altered in 1878 from sloop to ketch rig and re-registered as being 65 tons. Her owner at this time was George Williams. Later, after belonging for a few years to a Bristol timber merchant of the same name, she eventually came into the possession of Captain Alfred Williams of Llandogo. On the latter's death, just before the First World War, the trow remained on the shoal and slowly disintegrated.

BROCKWEIR

146 In the early 19th century, goods brought by water from the upper parts of the Wye were transhipped on to larger vessels bound for Bristol and various other destinations. The village was mainly inhabited by watermen engaged in this trade. At this time, there were a number of public houses in this small village and wages were often spent on drinking and cock fighting.

147 A striking feature of the present-day village is the Moravian church, situated on the left bank of the river. The name Moravian is derived from a group of Christians from Moravia who fled persecution in the 18th century. They came to Britain, in the 1730s, and established churches here. The church at Brockweir was erected, in 1832, on the site of the cockpit to which people had once come from far and wide. The cost of the building was shouldered chiefly by the Moravian congregation in Bristol.

TINTERN

148 This view shows the horseshoe bend made by the Wye at Tintern. On the left, in the background, is the railway bridge over the Wye near Tintern station. After crossing the river via this bridge, the Wye Valley Railway entered a tunnel, which took it through the narrow stretch of land opposite Tintern Abbey. It then carried on to Chepstow. The railway bridge no longer exists, but the Wireworks Bridge, on the right, is still a familiar sight in Tintern.

149 *Black's Guide to the Wye* of 1904 noted that the 'Tintern of tourists' was actually two villages, Tintern Parva and Chapel Hill, beside the abbey. These two settlements had grown together forming a 'long bow of houses' around the base of a wooded hill.

150 Top: This early 20th-century view of Tintern Abbey and village looks across the millpond. In the centre of the picture is the Abbey Stores, which, in 1901, was run by Edwin Ellis, grocer, draper and beer retailer. To the right is the *Royal George Hotel*, the proprietor of which, at this time, was Robert Hughes.

151 Centre: An aquatint of Tintern Abbey from William Gilpin's *Observations on the River Wye*, 1800. Dedicated to St Mary, Tintern Abbey was a Cistercian foundation whose mother house was the abbey of L'Aumone in Normandy. Cistercians lived a strict and austere life. They were known as 'white monks' because they wore habits made of undyed wool. Their abbeys were built in isolated places, away from habitation. For just over 400 years, the monks worked and prayed at Tintern Abbey, but it was suppressed in 1536 at the time of the Dissolution of the Monasteries. Then, Henry VIII gave the abbey and its estates to the Earl of Worcester. Subsequently the dukes of Beaufort became the owners.

152 Bottom: After the monastery was dissolved, the roofs of Tintern Abbey were stripped of their lead and, over the following centuries, the once-magnificent abbey and monastic buildings fell into decay. Visitors to Tintern in the late 18th and early 19th centuries found the ruins cloaked in ivy. Thomas Roscoe noted:

> The architecture is scarcely even defaced by time, but few columns having fallen; and the loss of these is partly hidden, and quite compensated for by the rich, heavy folds of Nature's most graceful drapery, luxuriant ivy, which adorns the lofty aisles and transepts of this majestic edifice, and scarcely suffers us to regret that it is a ruin.

The ivy, which was so attractive to these visitors to the abbey, was removed in the early 20th century.

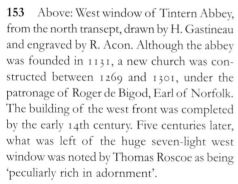

153 Above: West window of Tintern Abbey, from the north transept, drawn by H. Gastineau and engraved by R. Acon. Although the abbey was founded in 1131, a new church was constructed between 1269 and 1301, under the patronage of Roger de Bigod, Earl of Norfolk. The building of the west front was completed by the early 14th century. Five centuries later, what was left of the huge seven-light west window was noted by Thomas Roscoe as being 'peculiarly rich in adornment'.

154 Top right: Communication between each side of the river was once kept open by the ferry at Tintern Abbey, which was near the *Anchor Inn*. The ferry-boat waits at the bottom of the slipway in this early 20th-century view.

155 Right: Ferry arch, *c.*1905. Tourists wishing to visit the Devil's Pulpit, a high rock below Tintern, would cross the river by the ferry and climb up by a path through the woods. In 1901, Philip James was ferryman and boat owner here.

156　Charles Heath, writing in the early 19th century, was full of praise for the *Beaufort Arms* at Tintern, which was kept by Mr Mitchel who had the care of the abbey. Mrs Mitchel supplied refreshments for parties descending the Wye by boat and a tablecloth could be spread on the floor of the abbey for visitors to enjoy a repast in the cool shade of its walls. The inn had been 'fitted up in a neat and commodious manner', and several new rooms had been added, furnished with new beds and bedding. There was also a 'fresh stock of good liquors laid in their cellars'. In 1861, Mr and Mrs S.C. Hall spent a night at the *Beaufort Arms*, describing it as a 'humble, yet pleasant hostelrie'. By Edwardian times, the establishment was known as the *Beaufort Arms Hotel* or just *Beaufort Hotel* as the sign shows in this view dating from *c*.1908.

BANAGOR CRAGS

157　Visitors proceeding from Tintern to Chepstow, by water, would have had the advantage of seeing the rock formations along the river at close hand. Mr and Mrs S.C. Hall remarked that the boatmen would draw attention to 'the Devil's Pulpit, the Banagor Crags, the Twelve Apostles, St Peter's Thumb, The Lover's Leap, Wyntour's Leap, and so forth'. William Coxe wrote, 'The long line of Banagor Crags forms a perpendicular rampart on the left bank, wholly bare except where a few shrubs spring from the crevices or fringe their summits.' This view of the Banagor Crags is taken from Thomas Roscoe's *Wanderings and Excursions in South Wales*.

WYNDCLIFF

158 Top: The Wyndcliff is a steep limestone height, which rises over 800ft. from the river. This photograph of a four-horse coach below the Wyndcliff was taken on the road between Chepstow and Tintern. In the late 19th and early 20th centuries, a tourist coach called the *Eclis* was operated from Chepstow to Tintern. Along the way, the visitors could stop off at Moss Cottage in order to climb up the Wyndcliff.

159 Centre: According to Thomas Roscoe, Moss Cottage was a 'fanciful little habitation' about three miles from Tintern along the road to Chepstow. It had been built by the Duke of Beaufort, the owner of the Wyndcliff, to accommodate parties visiting the height. Mr and Mrs S.C. Hall mentioned that the cottage was also the residence of 'the care-taker of the hill' who would accompany parties to the top if needed. Each visitor was required to pay sixpence, a fee designed to be 'a barrier to prevent the intrusion of mere idlers from the town, who would disturb the tranquillity of the scene'.

160 Bottom: A path led up from Moss Cottage through the woods to the summit of the Wyndcliff. Charles Heath mentioned 'an irregular ascent of three hundred and sixty-three steps' where seats were placed in the prominent parts for both rest and enjoyment of the views. At the top of the Wyndcliff, visitors could enjoy a wonderful view. Thomas Roscoe included this illustration in his *Wanderings and Excursions in South Wales*. He observed:

> On gaining the open space, one of the most extensive and most beautiful views that can be imagined burst up on the eye … At a depth of about eight hundred feet, the steep descent below presents in some places single rocks; in others, a green and bushy precipice. In the valley, the eye follows for several miles the course of the Wye; which issues from a wooded glen on the left hand, curves around a green garden-like peninsula, rising into a hill studded with beautiful clumps of trees, then forces its foaming way, to the right, along a huge wall of rock, nearly as high as the point where you stand, and at length beyond Chepstow Castle, which looks like a ruined city, empties itself into the Bristol Channel, where ocean closes the dim and misty distance.

PIERCEFIELD

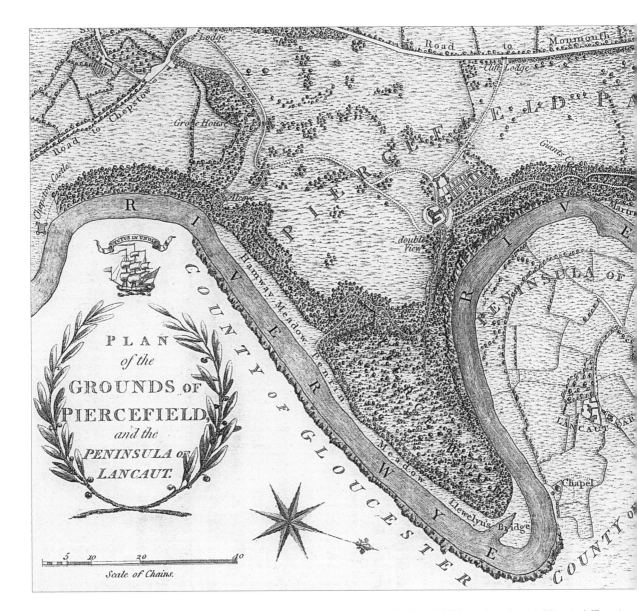

161 Plan of the grounds of Piercefield and the Lancaut peninsula from William Coxe's *An Historical Tour in Monmouthshire*. Portraying the scene, the author wrote:

> The grounds occupy an extensive space, stretching between the road and the Wy, from Wynd Cliff to the castle of Chepstow; and the walk leading from one extremity to the other, is scarcely less than three miles in length … The Wy, which is everywhere seen from a great elevation, passes between Wynd Cliff and the Banagor Rocks, winds around the peninsula of Lancaut, under a semicircular chain of stupendous cliffs, is lost in its sinuous course, again appears in a straighter line at the foot of the Lancaut rocks, and flows under the majestic ruins of Chepstow castle, towards the Severn.

The author added in a footnote:

> To view these delightful scenes, in full perfection, the traveller ought to visit the place at high tide, when the river is full; he should pass through the village of St Arvan's, to the upper part of the grounds, and descend from the Lover's Leap to the alcove, by which he will enjoy the whole scenery in proper succession, and to the greatest advantage.

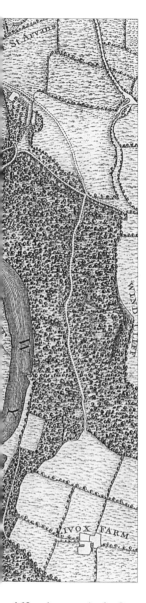

162 This view and description of Piercefield was included in *An Historical Tour in Monmouthshire* by William Coxe:

> The house is a magnificent building of freestone, seated nearly in the center of the park, and surrounded by lawns and open groves of wide spreading oak beech and elm. It stands on an elevation of ground that slopes gently to the banks of the Wy, and commands a distant and delightful view over the broad Severn and the red cliffs of Aust, backed by the fertile hills of Glocestershire; opposite appear the white rocks of Lancaut, which here lose their rugged form and harmonise with the surrounding scenery; beneath the castle and town of Chepstow present themselves to singular advantage, and the Wy sweeps in grand curves among rocks and woods, until it falls into the Severn.

163 An aquatint by Samuel Ireland entitled 'Chepstow &c. from Persfield'. The author wrote of a 'very extensive sketch that includes Chepstow Castle and the town beneath, together with the rocky cliffs designed as it were by nature to bound the course of the Wye, whose beautiful meandering extends to a distance of three miles, and then loses itself in the great waters of the Severn'.

TIDENHAM BEND

164 This early-20th century view of Tidenham Bend shows the grounds of Piercefield, in the central background, and the flat peninsula of Lancaut on the right. In the foreground, two trows are loading stone at the riverbank from one of the limestone quarries at the bend. According to Grahame E. Farr, a later trow which worked in this vicinity was the 58-ton *Palace*. She was purchased by Captain Giles Sims of Chepstow, in 1923, and carried stone from his quarry at Lancaut to the sea walls on the upper Bristol Channel and the River Severn until the start of the Second World War. In 1939, she was one of only two Severn trows still working under sail.

CHEPSTOW

165 Situated on the west bank of the River Wye, Chepstow Castle was built on a precipice overhanging the river. It has stood guard over a major river crossing for over 900 years. This print of the castle and bridge is from Thomas Roscoe's *Wanderings and Excursions in South Wales*. William fitz Osbern constructed the stone keep, shortly after the Norman Conquest. Then, over the centuries, additions and improvements were made to the castle up to the time of the Civil War and beyond. A name linked with the castle is that of the regicide, Henry Marten, who was among those who signed the death warrant of Charles I. He was imprisoned at the castle for 20 years until his death at the age of 78 years. The tower in which he was confined is called Marten's Tower.

166 In this view of Chepstow Castle, a trow is moored at Gwy Wharf, which was also known as Bridge Coal Wharf. She may have been the trow, *Alice*, used in the coal business of Thomas Sargent during the late 19th century, which was taken over, in 1896, by Edward Henry Weeks. Grahame E. Farr, in *Chepstow Boats*, recorded that *Alice* was built at Chepstow in 1868 by George Fryer.

167 Concerning Chepstow Bridge, William Coxe, in 1801, observed: 'The middle pier, a massive pillar of stone, separates the counties of Monmouth and Glocester; formerly all the other piers were of wood, but to avoid the expence of continual repairs, the county of Monmouth erected piers of stone, while those on the Glocestershire side still remain in their original state.' The author added, 'The floor of the bridge on the side of Glocestershire is supported by wooden piers, near 40 feet in height, resting on platforms of stone, which rise above the low water mark.'

168 The cast-iron bridge at Chepstow was designed by John Rastrick and erected by Hazledine, Rastrick and Co. of Bridgnorth. It was opened on 24 July 1816. Thomas Roscoe described the bridge as 'substantial and elegant, consisting of five iron arches, resting on stone piers. It is five hundred and thirty-two feet long: the centre arch is one hundred and ten feet, and the other two, on each side of it, seventy and fifty-four feet each in span.'

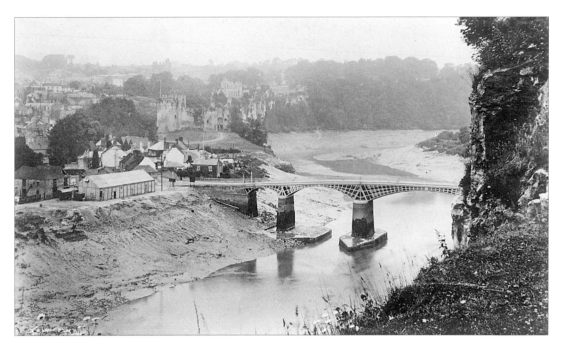

169 The rise and fall of the tide at Chepstow is remarkable. Steep mud banks and the foundations of the bridge have been revealed in this view at low tide, dating from *c.*1914. More than a century before this photograph was taken, William Coxe, with the assistance of his friend, Thomas Jennings, plumbed the river at high tide in early September. He found, 'The perpendicular height, from the bottom of the channel to the surface of the water, was 47 feet 3 inches' and noted that the tide at Chepstow was 'at an average 50 or 60 feet, and on some extraordinary occasions not less than 70'.

170 St Mary's Church originally belonged to the Benedictine priory established here in the 12th century. Over the years, the church has been much altered but one of its interesting features is the magnificent western entrance, which has an intricately decorated semi-circular arch with zigzag moulding.

171 The original name for Beaufort Square was just The Square. For centuries, it was the hub of life in the town, the large inclined area being the venue for both weekly markets and annual fairs. In the early years of the 20th century, the half-timbered building on the left was the premises of Mrs Hannah Griffiths, bookseller, stationer and printer. Later, this business was run by Miss Ellen Griffiths. Next door was butcher, James Jones. W. H. Smith & Son, booksellers, had a shop further up Beaufort Square and next to that was the *Bush Hotel*.

172 An early 20th-century view looking down High Street. On the right, at No. 8 High Street, is the hairdressing and tobacconist's shop established by Valentine Edward Watkins. At No. 9 is Bristol House, part of the drapery store operated by Herbert Lewis. The latter also ran his business from the building with the distinctive turret and the clock overhanging the street. On the left-hand side of the road is Skyrme's grocery store, at No. 28, and the premises of printer, Robert Quinton, at No. 26. The sign for E. Hurcum, butcher, can be seen at No. 25 High Street. In the background, on the left, is a granite drinking fountain, which was removed in 1919.

173 This Edwardian view of Chepstow looks up the High Street towards the Town Gate. In 1901, the shop on the extreme left, at No. 7, was that of watchmaker, John Gulliford. Next door, at No. 6, Mrs Margaret Ellen Cole was a saddler and harness maker. Thomas Harris, boot and shoemaker, was at No. 4, while William Woodgate had a provender and seed store at No. 4. The latter was a corn and flour factor besides being a provision and potato merchant. He also sold hay, straw and chaff and had other premises in the town. At No. 3 was the store of Edwin Ellis, grocer and ale and stout merchant. He had another shop at Abbey Stores, Tintern. A covered cart belonging to Edwin Ellis is in the background, on the right-hand side of the picture.

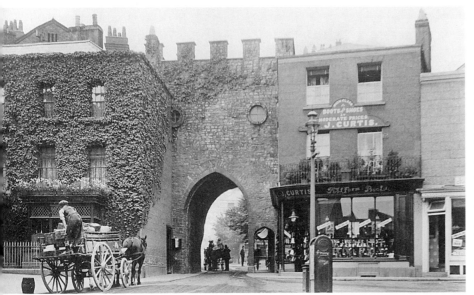

174 To the left of the Town Gate stands the Gate House at No. 1 High Street. The latter was rebuilt, in 1609, by widow, Margaret Cleyton, who was a benefactress to the town. To the right of the Town Gate, C.J. Curtis of 30 High Street once advertised 'High Class Boots & Shoes at Moderate prices' above his shop.

175 Originally constructed in the late 13th century, the Town Gate has undergone rebuilding over the centuries. It used to be the only way into Chepstow though the Port Wall, which stretched around the town to the river, and it was the place where market dues were collected. This view of the Town Gate, looking from Moor Street, dates from the 1920s. To the left of the arch is the shop of confectioner, Mrs Margaret Woods, with advertisements in the window for Ices and Fry's Chocolate. The *George Hotel*, to the right of the arch, had been one of Chepstow's main coaching inns. It was rebuilt in the late 1890s, having been severely damaged by fire. The shop at the corner, on the extreme left of this view, was the premises of J.A. Rymer, stationer and fancy draper.

176 The tubular suspension bridge, built to carry the railway line from Gloucester to Swansea and designed by Isambard Kingdom Brunel, was opened on 19 July 1852. It was 600ft. long with the main span being just over 300ft. This gave 50ft. of headroom for shipping, above the highest-recorded tide, and there was no need for piers to carry the bridge in the middle of the river. In 1962, the main span of the bridge was replaced by truss girders, positioned below the railway track. Now, the A48 road bridge crosses the river alongside the railway bridge.

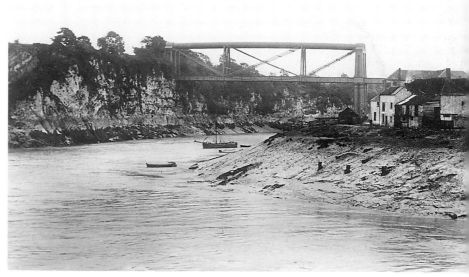

177 Entitled 'The New Railway Bridge, Chepstow', this engraving dates from c.1852. Besides depicting a train crossing the tubular railway bridge, a paddle steamer is shown travelling upstream to Chepstow. A trip across the Severn from Bristol, aboard a steam packet, was much favoured by tourists in the mid-19th century.

178 This aquatint from Samuel Ireland's *Picturesque Views on the River Wye* shows two trows moored at the Red Rocks below Chepstow. A small boat, full of passengers, is being rowed across the river. A man, coming from one of the trows and carrying a sack on his head, is presumably making for the waggon, which stands in front of the *Rock House Inn*. The author hoped, 'The annexed view of the Red Rocks, will give a general idea of the face of the river, in our passage down to the mouth of the Wye, where we found the tide uncommonly rapid, and where if the wind is brisk, the waters are troublesomely rough.'

Bibliography

Black's Guide to the Counties of Hereford & Monmouth (1873)

Black's Guide to the Wye (2nd edn. 1904)

Bradley, A.G., *The Wye* (2nd edn. 1926)

Burrow's Guide to the Wye from Source to Mouth (n.d)

Burton, Anthony, *The Wye Valley Walk* (1998)

Cash, J. Allan, *The River Wye* (1952)

Clew, Kenneth R., *Kilvert's Bredwardine* (2nd edn. 1980)

Cliffe, Charles Frederick, *The Book of South Wales, The Bristol Channel, Monmouthshire and the Wye* (1847)

Coxe, William, *An Historical Tour in Monmouthshire* (1801)

Crowe, Alan, *Bridges on the River Wye* (1995)

Druce, Fred, *Remembrance of Things Past: Ross on Wye 1869-1930* (1988)

Environment Agency, *Canoeists Guide to the River Wye* (1999)

Farr, Grahame E., *Chepstow Ships* (1954)

Fletcher, H.L.V., *Portrait of the Wye Valley* (1968)

Fosbroke, T.D., *The Wye Tour or Gilpin on the Wye with Picturesque, Historical and Archaeological Additions* (1822)

Gibbings, Robert, *Coming down the Wye* (1942)

Gilpin, William, *Observations on the River Wye and several parts of South Wales &c. relative chiefly to Picturesque Beauty* (5th edn. 1800)

Green, Colin, *Severn Traders* (1999)

Hadfield, Charles, *The Canals of South Wales and the Border* (2nd edn. 1967)

Hall, Mr and Mrs S.C., *The Book of South Wales, The Wye and the Coast* (1861)

Handley, B.M. and Dingwall, R., *The Wye Valley Railway and the Coleford Branch* (1982)

Heath, Charles, *Historical and Descriptive Accounts of the Ancient and Present State of the Town and Castle of Chepstow* (7th edn. 1821)

Heath Charles, *Historical and Descriptive Accounts of the Ancient and Present State of Tintern Abbey* (10th edn. 1827)

Heath, Charles, *The Excursion down the Wye from Ross to Monmouth* (8th edn. 1826)

Helme, Andrew, *Monmouth and The River Wye in Old Photographs from Goodrich to Brockweir* (1989)

Hurley, Heather, *Ross-on-Wye a photographic history of your town* (2002)

Hurley, Heather and Jon, *The Wye Valley Walk* (1994)

Ireland, Samuel, *Picturesque Views on the River Wye* (1797)

Jenkins, J. Geraint, *The Coracle* (1988)

Kelly's Directory of Herefordshire (1917)
Kelly's Directory of Monmouthshire (1891)
Kissack, Keith, *The River Wye* (1978)
Kissack, Keith, *Monmouth: The Making of a County Town* (1975)
Knight, Jeremy K., *Chepstow Castle* (1986)
Mason, Edmund J., *The Wye Valley: From River Mouth to Hereford* (1987)
Ordnance Survey Leisure Guide: Forest Of Dean And Wye Valley (1988)
Palmer, Roy, *The Folklore of Hereford & Worcester* (1992)
Palmer, Roy, *The Folklore of (old) Monmouthshire* (1998)
Palmer, Roy, *The Folklore of Radnorshire* (2001)
Pigot & Co.'s National Commercial Directory (1835)
Potts, W.H., *Roaming Down the Wye* (1949)
Rainsbury, Anne, *Chepstow and the River Wye in Old Photographs* (1989)
Ritchie, Leitch, *The Wye and its Associations: A Picturesque Ramble* (1841)
Robinson, David, *Tintern Abbey* (1986)
Roscoe, Thomas, *Wanderings and Excursions in South Wales including the Scenery of the River Wye* (n.d.)
Ross-on-Wye Visitor Handbook (1999)
Sale, Richard, *The Wye Valley* (1984)
Sandford, Anne, *Hereford in Old Photographs* (1987)
Sinclair, J.B. and Fenn, R.W.D., *Towns and Villages of Wales: Llanfair ym Muallt/Builth Wells* (1993)
Slater's National and Commercial Directory (1858-9)
Stockinger, Victor Richard, *The Rivers Wye and Lugg: A Documentary History 1555-1951* (1996)
The Illustrated Guide to the Banks of the Wye (n.d.)
The Official Guide to Monmouth and District (1936)
Twamley, Louisa Anne, *An Autumn Ramble by the Wye* (1839)
Ward Lock's The Wye Valley (n.d.)
Waters, Ivor, *About Chepstow* (1952)
Whitehead, David, *Yesterday's Town: Hereford* (1983)
Wye Valley Walk: Official Route Guide (n.d.)

CD Books
History, Topography and Directory of Herefordshire (1858, CD 2002)
Jakeman & Carver's Directory and Gazetteer of Herefordshire (1902, CD 2003)
Kelly's Directory of Gloucestershire (1902, 1906, 1910, CD 2002)
Kelly's Directory of Herefordshire (1909, CD 2003)
Kelly's Directory of Monmouthshire (1901, CD 2002)
Kelly's Directory of South Wales (1901, CD 2002, 1910, CD 2002)
Lewis, Samuel, *A Topographical Dictionary of England* (1831, CD 2003)
Lewis, Samuel, *A Topographical Dictionary of Wales* (1833, CD 2001)
Post Office Directory of Herefordshire (1879, CD 2002)
The Universal British Directory of Trade, Manufacture and Commerce (1791, CD 2001)
Wales Illustrated (1836, CD 2001)

Index

THE NORTH EAST PROSPECT OF